The Peace of Heaven

Hope for a Brighter Day

Dana Howard

The Peace of Heaven: Hope for a Brighter Day
Copyright © 2015 by Dana Howard

All scripture quotations are taken from the Holy Bible, New Living Translation copyright© 1996, 2004, 2007 by Tyndale House Foundation. Used by permission of Tyndale House Publishers Inc., Carol Stream, Illinois 60188. All rights reserved.

ISBN: 978-0-692-45556-2

Dedication

I dedicate this book to Robyn Ahearn, who encouraged me to write over the years. Many of the words of encouragement in this book were God's heart poured out through my hand when she needed a word of faith, hope, and love.

Contents

Foreword

*G*od wants to encourage you! There is such a passion in the heart of God to have His children full of hope and expectancy. No matter what has happened to you recently, God is more than able to restore your peace and bring you joy again. The dark clouds over our heads vanish when the living words of Christ enter our hearts. Yes, He wants you to be so full of courage and full of hope that you never visit the "caves of depression" again!

Both comforting and powerful words can be heard if you will be still… wait…and listen. God has much to say to you, words that can change the direction of your life. Simply stated, God loves you too much to leave you alone and let you suffer any longer. He has *hope* for you. Receive this living hope and it will bring you what Dana Howard has so wonderfully discovered—comfort for your soul!

All of us pass through valleys that are dark and foreboding. Life, indeed, does bring unexpected difficulties—the loss of a loved one, the loss of a job, the loss of good health. Most of us could use words of life that inspire and capture our hearts. You are about to read such words. The testing you have passed through will produce the triumph of hope if you don't give up or yield to your fear.

So many times in my life I needed to know that God is with me and that He hasn't given up on me. And so many times, the sweet words of life came to my soul and restored me, giving me strength for the journey that stretches out in front of us. People who carry hope are different. There is a light in their eyes, and a holy confidence.

Hope-filled lovers of God know the sound of His voice. He speaks, and we listen, and we are encouraged by His voice. Without the fresh breeze of heaven awakening our hearts, we so quickly get defeated and become convinced that God has forgotten us or that maybe He's too busy to care about what matters to us. Believe me, my friend, God is close to you this very moment and He promises to never, never leave you!

I'm so grateful to Dana Howard for this wonderful compilation of heaven's thoughts for you. It comes from her journey into God's endless love. As you read, think of the Lord sitting there near you, anxious for you to understand the wonders of this hope He extends to you.

The excitement you'll find in these pages comes from Dana spending many hours, even in the midst of her pain, finding the light of hope shining through the darkest cloud. The words she shares with us come from God's heart. It will delight you to read them. Read them out loud, listen to your own voice repeating His words, and let hope awaken inside of you. Dana has given us a treasure chest. Open it! Delight in what you see! Embrace every gem and make it your own. So open your heart to the voice of your Beloved as He speaks to you! It will change your life!

Dr. Brian Simmons
The Passion Translation Project

Preface: Homeless to Wholeness

I have always dreamed of a day where I could share the victory that God has brought in my life. God raised me up from a deep valley of despair and put my feet on solid ground. If He can do that for me, He can do that for everyone who puts their trust in Him. If you are in a hard place in your life, I know God will bring you through it. All you have to do is hold on to Him and He will bring you victory.

I lived through many years of an abusive relationship. From the verbal and physical abuse, to being alone with my baby while my husband spent time in jail, to having no money for food or gas, to our house being foreclosed on, to my husband having affairs and so much more, it was all more than I could handle.

Life was so stressful during that time that my mind snapped on more than one occasion and I was diagnosed with Bipolar Disorder, having to take medications daily. I struggled with deep depression and coped by sleeping the days away. All I had to hold on to was my relationship with Jesus. I spent many hours just staring at the picture of Jesus that hung on my wall as I cried out to the Lord for help.

The final straw was when my husband put his hands around my throat when I confronted him about the affair that he was having both during and after my pregnancy of my second son.

I went through a divorce and for the first time had to provide for myself and take care of my sons on my own. I gained weight rapidly due to stress and the medications I was taking and got close to 100 pounds more than I weigh today. I decided to go off my medications and that was the beginning of my life's most difficult trial.

I ended up in the hospital twice in a two month period of time due to a manic episode. While I was in the hospital, the power in my apartment had been shut off and my car was repossessed. After getting out of the hospital the second time I was still in a delusional state of mind. I packed up all my belongings in a U-Haul truck and drove away with a homeless man I had met when I was in the hospital. I had no idea where I was going and just started driving.

I found myself in Eureka, California and the man I was with traded all of my belongings for a beat up old car and abandoned the U-Haul truck in a parking lot. I was assaulted by the homeless man I was with one night even being strangled by a scarf to the point in which I could not breathe. I ran in fear for my life another night and the only thing I had to hold on to was a Scripture running through my head.

Out of fear, I got away from this homeless man and was all by myself. I found a place where I could get one meal a day and was on the streets with homeless people. I ate Kentucky Fried Chicken out of a dumpster. I carried around my pink little Bible as if it were my protection in the dark of the night where I was surrounded by strangers.

At the end of this journey I found myself pregnant and in a little motel in Willow Creek, California crying out to the Lord asking, "Why have You abandoned me when I put my trust in You?" I had a knock down drag out with God screaming at the top of my lungs only to end the conversation with, "Forgive me, Lord."

My mind started to clear from the mania and I traveled back home, nearly dying as my car rolled upside down into a ditch due to a hailstorm where my car spun out of control. If the car had spun in the other direction I would have gone off a cliff. God's hand of protection was over me so many times.

I made it back home and from my disability check I received from my employer I was able to rent a tiny little cottage. All I had was a blow-up mattress and a garbage bag full of clothes I had gotten at one of the homeless shelters in California. I remember the tears that rolled down my face that first night as I was so thankful to finally have a roof over my head and a place to call home.

I was pregnant and didn't know if I should give my baby up for adoption because of my illness. In the end I couldn't bear the thought of giving up my child. All seemed well until my baby boy was three months old and I had another manic episode. I fell asleep at the wheel at 50 miles an hour and my car flew in the air into a field. Neither my son nor I were injured.

I got out of a three week stay in the hospital and cried out to God asking Him what I should do. At that moment, I knew in my heart of hearts that I needed to give my baby up for adoption because I was not well. I called my church's pastor's wife and she found out that the music pastor and her husband wanted to adopt my son.

Fast forward seven years and this is the miracle of God's grace, mercy, and restoration. I have a great job that I have had for ten years (minus the two years I was on leave of absence during my illness). My oldest son graduated from high school last spring and has started his own business. I got remarried to a wonderful man two years ago and we are raising my second son together who is eleven years old. Thousands of dollars of debt that was incurred when I got sick has been paid off. My husband and I purchased our first home together a year ago.

I have not had another manic episode or deep bout of depression. My son who was adopted and is now seven years old is very much a part of my life. He calls me Auntie Dana. Just last Christmas when I dropped off a gift at his house he exclaimed, "I love you, Auntie Dana!" and gave me a big hug. His mom has become a dear friend of mine and I didn't even know her prior to her adopting my son.

I share this with all of you today as a witness to God's amazing love. Even in my darkest hours, he was always there. When I feel down on myself or discouraged, He always lifts me up and covers me with His words of love and compassion. It is amazing to me that finally after all those years of trials and tribulations my life actually seems normal. It is a season of peace and I am so thankful for that.

No matter what you're going through, God's love never fails. I encourage you to sit down one day and write down on a piece of paper, "Dear Son or Daughter," and see what God would like to share with you. I promise you that what God wants to share with you is His perfect love.

Psalm 30:2
O Lord my God, I cried to you for help,
and you restored my health.

Introduction

*T*he *Peace of Heaven* was birthed out of adversity. It came through years of enduring trials that nearly cost me my life. Out of the ashes came this book written for those who could use words of hope, love, and encouragement to walk into a future filled with blessings that come from God. His peace is awaiting you as you come to spend time in His presence.

There are so many lost and broken hearts in this world and I believe that all of us, from one time to another, need that voice of encouragement to help us make it through our days, which can oftentimes be filled with trials and tribulations. *The Peace of Heaven* is a book that will fill you with hope and encouragement and help you embrace the great and amazing love of God. It will inspire you to draw closer to Him through your daily walk of life.

Years ago, when I was at a Christian women's retreat, the speaker asked us to take out a piece of paper and write on the top, "Dear Daughter." He asked us to write down what we felt that God was sharing with us.

It was in that moment that the floodgates of heaven opened up. It was as if a dam burst open and my pen took to paper with words pouring out one after another. As I poured my heart out to Him on paper, He would respond in loving kindness. I could barely keep up with the thoughts that were taking shape into a love letter that was the beginning of a new way I could communicate with God—listening and allowing God to share His love with me through writing.

I came home and typed up those words, printed them out on fancy paper, and bound them in a folder. It felt like one of the greatest gifts I had ever received. I felt loved of God. I felt special. I had received a treasure that deeply touched my heart. This was something I could read and reread whenever I needed love and encouragement.

Following that experience, for days on end I would sit and write in journals words that I believed were pouring out from the heart of God.

I then began to write words of encouragement from the Lord for others, which is where the journey of writing this book began.

The times I write are precious moments I spend with the Lord. I quietly listen to that still, small voice and words of hope, love, and encouragement pour out as if they are coming straight from the heart of God.

There are many ways the Lord speaks to us. This book is simply an expression of the love that I believe God holds in His heart for each and every one of us. His love for us is profound. Writing from the perspective of Jesus talking to you gives me a creative way to express God's love for His children.

It is with great joy that I share with you *The Peace of Heaven* that I believe was inspired by the heart of God. Just sit back and soak in His love as you read. You may read a writing one day and notice certain things speak to you on that day. Then you might revisit that same writing down the road and feel like you are reading it for the first time.

It is my prayer that these words lift your spirit and bring hope to your heart. This book is my gift back to God in the hope that you are blessed with the love that God has poured out over me throughout the years. You are so loved by God. May your faith in God bring you *The Peace of Heaven*!

Love in Christ,

Dana Howard

Hebrews 11:1
Faith is the confidence that what we hope for will actually happen; it gives us assurance about things we cannot see.

1. *A Love Letter from the King to a Broken Heart*

Dearest Beloved Child,

I know and understand your pain. I want to thank you personally for your faithfulness to me. You are building up storehouses of treasuries in the heavens every time you call upon my name, every time you sing my praises while you walk through the storms of life. Rest your weary head upon my shoulders and I will comfort you.

You are chosen, my Beloved, for a purpose far greater than you could ever imagine. What you bear here on earth by grace through me will be multiplied infinitely as unspeakable joy in heaven. This life you live is a blip on the screen, a blink of the eye in comparison to your eternal resting place where you will be free of heartache, pain, and discomfort. Eternally you will experience unfathomable peace and ultimate freedom. Keep this in mind during your sufferings.

I am here to bring you new hope this day. It will not always be this difficult. You are in the Refiner's Fire. I am purifying your heart and washing you with holiness.

You are my dearest beloved treasure and I call you friend. I can trust in your faithfulness toward me and this will take you far in my kingdom.

I will lift you up to a brighter day. Just continue to press into me and you will make it through. In time, you will hardly be able to remember how difficult it has been for you. I will lead you to a place of freedom and mend any brokenness within you.

I send you my love this day. Reach out and receive it. You are forever in my arms. I love you beyond compare.

With Love,

Your Jesus

Isaiah 48:10
I have refined you, but not as silver is refined.
Rather, I have refined you in the furnace of suffering.

2. Seek After Me

*I*n the night hours, as you call upon my name, I come running to you. As you awake each morning, the sound of my name upon your lips brings my heart great joy. I want you to know that I consider you my dearest friend, a confidant, one I can share the mysteries of the heavens with as you earnestly seek my face.

I want you to understand new things about my love for you. I want you to understand the deepness of my love for you. My love for you has no bounds—it is limitless. As far as the eye can see is but a glance in comparison to the vast universe of love I offer to you through my Son.

It is through my Son that you have been given new life. It is through my Son's sacrifice on the cross that you have been given a new lease on life, a new opportunity to walk in grace, dignity, and ultimate freedom.

Release all your fears and doubts to me and I will pour out upon you life-giving words of wisdom that will empower you to walk through your days victoriously. Call upon the name of Jesus, and you shall see walls fall down before you. Call upon the name of Jesus, and you shall see the heavens open up and bring in the new rains of healing and restoration.

Be hopeful. Look forward, not behind. You cannot do anything about what happened yesterday, but you can do something new today. You can bring light into this world through me. You are a great light to the world for I am in you and I am light.

Seek after me and I will give my all unto you. I will make a way where there seems to be no way. I will part the seas for you and you will walk in a new land with new and greater opportunities to serve your King.

Be confident that you have what it takes to be victorious. You have your God on your side. There is nothing that can thwart the plans I have for your life. I have a perfect purpose for your life. Seek after me and I will reveal it to you. Know that as you are seeking after me you are always moving forward and never behind.

I am at your side at all times and in all circumstances. You are never alone. I am with you always.

> *Deuteronomy 4:29*
> *But from there you will search again for the Lord your God. And if you search for him with all your heart and soul, you will find him.*

3. I Show Myself to You in Many Ways

My Beloved, I call you friend. You can call me friend too. I desire a personal, intimate relationship with you. I want to be your best friend. I want to be your confidant. You can always count on me to listen to you. I will respond in loving kindness. Though you may not hear my voice, I am ever present before you. I show myself to you in many ways.

Be open to my wisdom that I will impart to you as you come and spend time with me. You will find that as you take the time to be in fellowship with me, your burdens will be lightened and you will receive new strength and a renewed spirit.

I am molding you into my image and likeness so that you are a reflection of me to others whom I place along your path. Your story will bring hope to others who are lost and broken for they will be witness of the miraculous ways I have moved in your life because of the close friendship we share. Others will desire the same closeness to me and that will draw them into my heart in a new way.

Let my light of love shine through you to others. I will be the hope you need to make it through your day. My Friend, I love you.

John 14:21
Those who accept my commandments and obey them
are the ones who love me. And because they love me,
my Father will love them. And I will love them and
reveal myself to each of them.

4. I Will Pull You out of the Quicksand and Place Your Feet upon the Rock

*M*y Child, I care deeply for you and value who you are inside. I see what you are going through, what you have been through, and what you are going to go through. In the past I have been with you. In the present I am with you. And in the future I will be with you. There is not one thought of yours that goes unnoticed by me—not one cry that escapes my ears.

I know at times you can have battles in your thought life. At times you are not happy with yourself and are not happy with your life. You do not have to remain stuck in your current circumstances.

Does life sometimes make you feel like you are being swallowed up in quicksand and you can't find anyone to help pull you out? Know that when you are caught in a situation that is pulling you under—I will always provide a way for you to return to solid ground. I will pull you out of the quicksand as you lift up your hand and heart to me. There is always a way out when I am in your life.

As you come to me in prayer over your current circumstances, seek my wisdom and I will give you new insight into any problem you may be facing. As I reveal to you truths about your situation, your mind will be opened to new ideas and creative ways for you to rise up and find solid ground. Sometimes I will speak these things to your inner man. Sometimes I will send others your way to speak into your life.

However I choose to bless you with answers, just continue to put your hope and trust in me, and I will pull you out of the quicksand and set your feet upon the Rock. I am your firm foundation, and as you stand upon the Rock you cannot be shaken.

Be confident in this—I have called you here this day. I have chosen you. I have a great purpose for your life. Seek after me and I will reveal it to you. My blessing I rest upon you this hour.

Go now and breathe in my peace. I will fill you up with new joy that is coming down upon you from the heavens.

Psalm 40:2
He lifted me out of the pit of despair, out of the mud
and the mire. He set my feet on solid ground and
steadied me as I walked along.

5. I Will Make a Way for You in the Wilderness

When your heart reaches out to me I am reaching out to you. I extend to you all of my love, all of my compassion, and all of my grace. In times of trouble do not be afraid for I am with you. The road before you may appear treacherous, but remember—you are not alone.

We will take it one step at a time, and before you know it you will be resting in green meadows, basking in the glory of my light. I am always with you to guide you down the right path. Take time to come away and be with me. This will refresh your spirit and bring joy to your heart on even the most difficult of days.

Be patient and trust in me. I will make a way for you in the wilderness and you shall be set free.

Psalm 23:1-2
The Lord is my shepherd; I have all that I need. He lets me rest in green meadows; he leads me beside peaceful streams.

6. I Am a Place of Refuge for You

*I*n your darkest hours, I am there. In the midst of your pain, I am there. When you think you can't make it through another day, I am there. My love surrounds you and protects you from harm.

Release it all to me—your thoughts, your cares, your hurts. I will take them from you to lift the burden from your shoulders as you come to spend time with me.

I have many ways of lightening your load that will bring you rest and comfort. When you are too exhausted to even talk to me, just focus your heart on me and I will hold you in my arms.

I am a place of refuge for you—a place where you feel safe and protected. I want to bring you the comfort your heart is longing for. It does not take a lot of effort to come to me, and there is such a great reward for you when you do.

When you are anxious about how all the details of the day are going to work out, trust in me. Do not fear for I will be with you all the way. I will go before you and orchestrate things on your behalf for the good of all my children.

 Seek after me and you will find me—even in places you were not expecting. I am near you.

2 Samuel 22:31
God's way is perfect. All the Lord's promises prove true.
He is a shield for all who look to him for protection.

7. I Will Love You Through This

My Sweet and Tender Heart, I stand right by your side this day and all of your days. When times are uncertain, know that I am here to bring you comfort and strength. As you lift up all your worries and concerns to me, I will take them from you to bring you peace.

Let the fire of my love bring you new insight and understanding into the ways I am working within your life despite the trials and tribulations. I will love you through this. What you are walking through right now will not break you but will make you stronger and bring you into an even deeper relationship with me.

Take hold of my hand and let me lead you beside still waters. You are an overcomer and this is a new opportunity for your strength in me to be an encouragement to others who are also going through the same trials.

Stand strong. Be still before me. I am with you.

Psalm 23:6
*Surely your goodness and unfailing love will pursue
me all the days of my life, and I will live in the house
of the Lord forever.*

8. *You Are Precious in My Eyes*

My Sweet and Precious Child—I am with you today. I am right by your side whispering softly to your spirit to help you process through your thoughts and concerns. I will pour out my wisdom upon you so that you have better direction on how you should proceed.

You have a kind and caring heart with which I am well pleased. I know that at times the anguish of your heart overwhelms you. I know that at times you feel as though you can't make it through one more day. I know that you have difficulty understanding why it is taking so long for the promises I speak of to be fulfilled in your life.

It is all part of a process of learning and growing so that you can get to a state of total freedom, so that nothing will get in the way of the life-giving relationship that I share with you. I am not delayed in answering your prayers. I am right on time.

Stand strong in your faith and you will be overwhelmed with the blessings you will receive in times to come. In the present time, rest in my love and continue to give your best each day. I will always bring blessings your way and open your eyes to a greater understanding and awareness of all I am doing in your life.

You are precious in my eyes. Enjoy your day and remember I am standing right by your side.

Daniel 10:19
"Don't be afraid," he said, "for you are very precious
to God. Peace! Be encouraged! Be strong!"
As he spoke these words to me, I suddenly felt stronger
and said to him, "Please speak to me, my lord, for you
have strengthened me."

9. *I Will Always Be Faithful to You*

*B*e near me as I am near you. Stand with me as I stand with you. As you search your heart, you will find within it the greatest treasure—my Spirit. I breathe new life into you each day as you reach out to me and call upon my name.

Oh, my Darling Child, you honor me when you hold gratitude in your heart for the things I do for you, for the little gifts I send your way just because I love you. Thank you for your thankful heart. What great joy I receive when my children appreciate the love I give in many different ways.

Seek me in all that you do and you will find even more reasons to be thankful. In this way as your spirit connects with mine, you will be uplifted up with an enthusiasm to share with others what I have to offer—complete and unfailing love. I will be faithful to you always. This you can count on.

Deuteronomy 7:9
Understand, therefore, that the Lord your God is indeed God. He is the faithful God who keeps his covenant for a thousand generations and lavishes his unfailing love on those who love him and obey his commands.

10. I Have Called You According to My Purpose

*M*y Beloved, I look upon you and think to myself what a perfect creation you are. I know the intents of your heart, my Child. I see that you are making your best effort at trying to lead a holy and righteous life. Just relax and rest in me. Let me lighten your load and the expectations you put upon yourself for perfection.

When I see you this day and every day, I behold perfection before my very eyes. You have no idea how greatly you please my heart. You cannot even begin to comprehend how very proud I am of you right now for fervently calling out to me. You may think you do all the talking but I also see you as a great listener as you seek to hear my voice.

I am your friend, the best and truest you will ever know. You will behold me face to face one day. That is my promise to you. I am giving you the rest you need to recharge your batteries so that you can complete the task I have laid before you.

Just as you were pleasantly surprised the other day, I will surprise you again in even greater ways. Allow me to fill in the blanks, the missing pieces. I will give you each and every one of them as they are needed, right on time. My love for you reaches the heavens and will never cease. I have always loved you and have called you according to my purpose.

Stay the course and you will be well pleased just as I am well pleased with you. Go now and bask in the presence of my Father tonight and you shall find rest. My peace will fall upon you. I love you.

Romans 8:28
And we know that God causes everything to work together for the good of those who love God and are called according to his purpose for them.

11. I Am Your Shelter During the Storms

*D*earest Beloved Child, when you are standing at a crossroad in your life and do not know which way to turn—call upon my name. It may be unclear to you now, but I will make the way for you. Do not fear that you will stumble and fall for I am here to protect you.

I am the calm within your spirit when times are rough. I am your shelter during the storms that can rage about you throughout your days. It will not always be difficult even though it may seem like the battle you are in is never-ending. I have come so that you may have rest.

Psalm 91:1
Those who live in the shelter of the Most High will
find rest in the shadow of the Almighty.

12. Stand Upon My Word

G uard your heart and mind from the attacks of the enemy by proclaiming the truth in my Word. Stand upon my Word and rejoice for within it lies my glorious promises for your life.

Receive my abundant love this day. If you are feeling weak, rest in my arms and I will give you strength. Let my words be the hope that fills your heart with gladness.

Psalm 119:89

Your eternal word, O Lord, stands firm in heaven.

13. I Am Working on Your Behalf

R est in me. Bring all of your thoughts, concerns, and anxieties and lay them at my feet. Submit yourself to me and I will lead you down the right path. Do not weary. The path may seem long and burdensome at times but I am with you. You are not alone in this.

Let my love strengthen you. I will keep you safe from harm and set up a hedge about you that keeps you walking down the path that leads to freedom, insight, and new revelation into my goodness. Trust in me. Know that I am working on your behalf and trailblazing the way for you to walk in truth and righteousness.

Seek me and you shall find me even in places you were not expecting. I will be a light to you as you go forth into this new day. Rest in me. I am right by your side.

Job 8:6
***And if you are pure and live with integrity, he will
surely rise up and restore your happy home.***

14. I Am Refining Your Spirit and Transforming Your Mind

S weet Child, let me wrap my loving arms around you. Soak in my Spirit within as you rest in me. I am with you today. Your confidence is in me and comes through me. You have a light within you that permeates the darkness. I am that light. I am your light.

Some days you will be frustrated by the events of the day. All you need to do is continue to press into me. There is no victory without a battle.

I am refining your spirit and transforming your mind. Do not weary when the challenges of the day fall upon your shoulders. You do not carry them alone although it may seem so at times.

Remember, I am training you for battle. I am teaching you how to be victorious. My Word will come alive within you as you call upon my name. Go forth and take new territory! The greater the battle, the greater the victory!

Romans 12:2
Don't copy the behavior and customs of this world, but let God transform you into a new person by changing the way you think. Then you will learn to know God's will for you, which is good and pleasing and perfect.

15. My Love Is Sovereign and Unyielding

*B*eloved Child, my love is one of the universe's greatest mysteries. I love all of my children equally, for each child is my masterpiece created out of the same love, the purest kind of love. My love is sovereign and unyielding. It is fathomless.

Love shows itself in many different ways. For some, love is experienced in great measure. For others, love has been fleeting. My love for you never changes. My love is with you always.

My Child, you must remember that this is a fallen world trying to make its way back home. As the end draws near, the fight for good and evil will become stronger and stronger. It is not I who oppresses but he who is in the world. The enemy would have it that all would perish. But I, out of my sovereign love, have overcome the world.

What truly matters is not what you experience now in your life. What truly matters is what you will behold in the life to come. Eternal life. You need not understand why life is so complex. All you need to do is to have faith in me.

I am the Savior of all. All who believe in me will experience a measure of blessing that is truly out of this world. That measure is saved for those who believe in me and have put their trust in me.

I bless you with just one parting truth this day. No matter where you are in life or what you are experiencing, the truth is that I love you. Yes, you are and always will be loved by the one who gave you life.

Psalm 109:21
But deal well with me, O Sovereign Lord, for the sake of your own reputation! Rescue me because you are so faithful and good.

16. Love Me with All of Your Heart

O h, how I love you! I pour out my grace upon you this day. How is it that you could fully live without my mercy? It would be impossible for you to grow in true love without my grace. Continue to seek after me.

What is your purpose in life? What is your true calling? To love me with all of your heart, with all of your soul, with all of your strength, and with all your mind. And yes, to love others as you love yourself. Hope in me, my Child, and know that your hope in me will not disappoint you.

The trials that you go through are helping you to mature and grow you in love. I am your master just as you are my servant. I am the greatest teacher you will ever know. I am teaching you how to love the way I love you.

Come to me even when you are weary and I will give you rest. Delight in me and I will give you the desires of your heart!

Luke 10:27
The man answered, "'You must love the Lord your God with all your heart, all your soul, all your strength, and all your mind.' And, 'Love your neighbor as yourself.'"

17. I Will Guide Your Every Step

My Dear Child, you are brave indeed. You have boldly taken on new challenges that I have placed before you. As you continue to put your trust in me and seek my guidance, I will be with you to help you endure any trials that come your way. I will help you to overcome your challenges and will propel you forward to places you have never even dreamed of.

I want to show you my goodness and my faithfulness. I know that you are seeking my promise, and I want you to rest assured that the time is drawing nearer than you can imagine. Enjoy the journey. You will be able to look back on the trials of your journey and come to understand why I allowed you to go through them.

You were not only called to be my servant, you were called to be my Bride. You will stand before me in righteousness, purity, and wholeness with the fullness of my Spirit within you. Continue to press into me as you have been doing. Seek after my truth and I will guide your every step and give you great knowledge and understanding of my love for you and why I suffered on the cross for you.

I am pleased with you and look upon you with great love and admiration. I am proud of you. Keep steadfast and true to my calling for your life that I will reveal to you in the days to come.

Rest now and be comforted in my presence. New joy will be with you when you arise. A new day is dawning and my angels will be watching over you as you rest in peace.

Exodus 15:13
With your unfailing love you lead the people you have redeemed. In your might, you guide them to your sacred home.

18. I Will Carry You

My Humble Child, be not weary for I am your helper in times of need. I have not forgotten you. You are always on the forefront of my mind. You cannot always see the end from the beginning, but know this—my plans for you are wonderful. What you are lacking now you will be overflowing with in times to come.

My arms are around you this day to comfort, to guide and protect you. Try your best to not let the enemy's lies bring you down. He will try to overwhelm you with thoughts of inadequacies and failures. These are lies. The truth is that you are my child for whom all my goodness flows.

You are full of my goodness and my grace is sufficient for you even on days when you are heavy laden and sorrowful. I hear the cries of your heart and my heart is filled with compassion for you. My love for you abounds. You are a precious soul, so perfectly created by me. You are the apple of my eye.

All will be well, my Beloved. You are esteemed in the kingdom of heaven and I have called you to higher ground. You have been walking up the steep mountain path and the journey has been wearisome. As you continue to draw on my strength, I will carry you the rest of the way up the mountain. From the top you will look below and will come to understand how I have been cultivating your heart in holiness.

From the mountain top you will see things as you have never seen them, and all that you have learned on this rocky, steep path will bubble over and pour out as wisdom that will empower you to bring healing to those who are lost and broken.

The end of this path is in sight. It only takes a gust of wind to move the clouds that block your view of the mountain top. My Spirit is blowing gently and perfectly upon your path. You will behold my majesty in new and creative ways in days to come.

Draw into my arms and let me shelter you. I have come so that you may have rest. I bring peace and help to you this day. All will be well. I love you.

Psalm 28:9
Save your people! Bless Israel, your special possession.
Lead them like a shepherd, and carry them in your
arms forever.

19. I Am Holding On to You

I stand beside you this night to listen to you, to hear your thoughts. There is no time or place that I am not with you. I am with you always. You may have lost your footing for a moment and slipped. You are going to be just fine, for I am holding on to you.

Just because you have stumbled does not mean you have fallen. On the contrary, this incident has served its purpose to bring you back into my arms where you belong. I have been patiently waiting for your arrival. All you need to do is knock and I will open up the door to my heart where we can discuss your circumstances in the safety of my loving presence.

I cherish you and am so proud to call you my Beloved Child. You have not disappointed me. The fact that you are with me now brings great joy to my heart. I have been waiting for this special moment in time to speak directly to your spirit.

My love for you abounds, my Child. Never forget the fact that I never forget about you. You are always in my heart and on my mind.

Rest this night in the comfort of my love. I will be with you as you sleep and will greet you when you arise in the morning. I will be with you tomorrow and will help you. Sweet dreams, my Child.

Deuteronomy 11:22-23
Be careful to obey all these commands I am giving you. Show love to the Lord your God by walking in his ways and holding tightly to him. Then the Lord will drive out all the nations ahead of you, though they are much greater and stronger than you, and you will take over their land.

20. I Will Give You What You Need

*A*s you reach out to me in prayer, I am reaching out to you. Do not worry about how every little detail is going to work out. The tapestry of your life is being woven by me, and even the tiniest piece of thread is not overlooked but strategically placed exactly where it needs to be.

Allow me to tend to the details for you. Simply trust in your Provider and I will give you what you need, exactly how and when you need it.

Be mindful to rest in me. Keep your hope alive within you by proclaiming my promises that I speak of so many times in my Word. When you speak these truths they will manifest in your life in the perfect time—not too late, not too early.

I am a God of perfection and I am weaving my glory and promises into the tapestry of your life each day. Stay the course and keep your eyes fixed on me. I am making the way for you. Victory is in the making and joy is on its wings!

2 Peter 1:3
By his divine power, God has given us everything
we need for living a godly life. We have received all
of this by coming to know him, the one who called
us to himself by means of his marvelous glory and
excellence.

21. Sit at My Feet

S it at my feet and listen to me. Listen to the gentle words of love that I pour upon you this hour. As you receive my love, be open to the transformational powers of my undying love for you.

It is not my perfect plan that you should struggle or battle through life, but that is the way of the world. It is my perfect plan that you continue to put your faith and trust in me. By doing that, my Spirit will come alive within your heart and you will reap the benefits that I pour out upon my children who believe in me.

I am with you today and all of your days.

Luke 10:38-39
As Jesus and the disciples continued on their way
to Jerusalem, they came to a certain village where a
woman named Martha welcomed him into her home.
Her sister, Mary, sat at the Lord's feet, listening to
what he taught.

22. My Light Is upon You

*D*earest Child, I beckon you to call upon my name. Come before me so that I may see your face. Let me uncover your hurts and pains and bring you comfort that is true and lasting.

You may be facing something today that is greater than what you thought you could handle. This is the battle of life. Some days you will feel stronger than others. Today, remember that when you are weak, I am strong. I will carry you through this dark hour and bring you to the other side that is full of light and hope.

You are much stronger than you think you are. I have overcome so that you too may overcome. My light breaks through the darkness and casts away shadows and things lurking in dark corners. My light is upon you.

Let me be your strength, the strength that carries you through the day. I am with you.

Isaiah 60:1
Arise, Jerusalem! Let your light shine for all to see.
For the glory of the Lord rises to shine on you.

23. *The Depth of My Love*

O h, that you would know the depth of my love for you! My love for you is fathomless. It is incomprehensible. It is so great that I created a universe that is never ending just to give you a glimpse of the love I hold in my heart just for you. And yet, even a never-ending universe cannot contain my love.

My love for you is infinite. My heart is infinite and contains so much love that I created time without end so that I could love you for eternity. My love for you will never cease.

Your comprehension of my love is like one grain of sand in ten thousand planets, yet that does not even begin to compare to the love I hold in my heart for you. You are never outside of my love.

When you do not feel my love, it is not because it is not there. My love for you is constant. My love was, is, and ever shall be. Although you are limited in your understanding of how much I love you, know that I do.

I do all things out of love for you. Just as you cannot comprehend the depths to which I love you, you will not always understand why I do what I do. Just know and remember, as I speak of in my Word, that my thoughts are higher than your thoughts and my ways are higher than your ways. What I do, I do because I love you.

Today, as you ponder on my love, rest assured that I will give you what you need to make it through the day no matter what it holds. Hold on to this one thought today—I love you.

Ephesians 3:16-21
I pray that from his glorious, unlimited resources he will empower you with inner strength through his Spirit. Then Christ will make his home in your hearts as you trust in him. Your roots will grow down into God's love and keep you strong. And may you have the power to understand, as all God's people should,

how wide, how long, how high, and how deep his love is. May you experience the love of Christ, though it is too great to understand fully. Then you will be made complete with all the fullness of life and power that comes from God. Now all glory to God, who is able, through his mighty power at work within us, to accomplish infinitely more than we might ask or think. Glory to him in the church and in Christ Jesus through all generations forever and ever! Amen.

24. I Am Standing with You

S tand strong, my Child! I am your covering. I am your protective shield. You are not alone in this battle. I am standing with you. When you feel lost, call upon my name. When you feel afraid, come and hide in my arms. When you feel bewildered, seek my Word. My truth shall make a way for you always—the way of righteousness.

Psalm 73:23
Yet I still belong to you; you hold my right hand.

25. The Fire of My Love Protects You from Harm

*T*he fire of my love burns within your heart this day to give you strength. The fire of my love protects you from harm. It keeps the pestilence out and refines your walk toward holiness.

As the fire of my love is all around you, you are empowered to stand strong against the enemy so that you are able to live a life that is full of my riches and wealth. The kind of wealth that I speak of is the riches that are stored in the treasury of your heart where I reside.

I make deposits into the treasury of your heart each time you call upon my name, every time you reach out to someone in need, every moment you spend in worship before the Father.

Let the fire of my love light your heart on fire with love and passion for the one who has given you life. I have come so that you may have life and have it in abundance.

Psalm 5:11
But let all who take refuge in you rejoice; let them
sing joyful praises forever. Spread your protection
over them, that all who love your name may be filled
with joy.

26. You Are an Overcomer through Me

O h, great joy you are to my heart! Look at all that I am doing in your life. You are an overcomer through me. It takes effort on your part to be an overcomer, and with your effort comes my blessing.

Strive to do your very best, to give all you have, to pour your heart into the lives of others whom I have put in your midst. As I bring those people to you, I will also give you the wisdom you need to bring hearts closer to me and, for some, to bring them into my heart for the very first time.

I am working within you to bring life to others through me. Take another step with me on your journey today and count this day as a victory. Rejoice, for tomorrow will be another day of victory as you put all your trust in me.

John 16:33
I have told you all this so that you may have peace in me. Here on earth you will have many trials and sorrows. But take heart, because I have overcome the world.

27. *Your Future Will Be Brighter than Your Past*

Y ou are a walking testimony that does not hold back from pouring hope into the lives of others. Every prayer uttered by your lips and said quietly within your heart is heard by me. I am a God who answers those who are faithful and diligent in their pursuit of holiness.

Wisdom—sweet, beautiful wisdom—it is yours. All you need to do is ask.

Over and over I have heard the cries of your heart. Your years of hardship were not in vain. Your future will be brighter than your past. Let your hope stand strong. I am not a God who will disappoint. I may not answer in your timing, but in my perfect timing.

My plans for you are perfect and each answer is delivered at the perfect time. Sing unto my heart and I will sing unto your heart.

Rest in my love for it is yours and I give it to you pressed down, shaken together, and overflowing.

Haggai 2:9
The future glory of this Temple will be greater than its
past glory, says the Lord of Heaven's Armies. And in
this place I will bring peace. I, the Lord of Heaven's
Armies, have spoken!

28. Keep Your Eyes Focused on Me

This day, lift up your heart to me. I take your heart in my hand and cleanse it with my love. As my love cleanses your heart, your spirit will be refreshed and you will walk again in purity before me.

Keep your eyes focused on me and I will be your great reward. Remember, as you have asked for forgiveness, I have cleansed your heart. You are free.

Go now and rejoice, for it is a new day. Expect the miraculous. I have so much to give to you. Open your heart to receive my love and you will be greatly blessed.

Psalm 80:3
Turn us again to yourself, O God. Make your face
shine down upon us. Only then will we be saved.

29. You Are Always a New Creation in Me

*D*earest Child, you are the beloved of my heart. I long to give you all the desires of your heart. I long to see you grow deeper and deeper in love with me. My love for you is deep and wide. My mighty hand is upon you.

I stand before the throne of my Father, pleading on your behalf that you will always be keen to heed my voice—to make right choices in the midst of a fallen world. When you are with me, you are on the right path that leads to righteousness and holiness.

I will quiet the noises that distract you. I will place a muffle upon your ears that creates a cushion and has a dampening effect to the many voices that can easily toss you to and fro. You will hear my voice loud and clear without distraction. My voice will lead you gently throughout your days and will keep you pliable to the molding and transformational power of my love.

When you are in doubt, listen to my voice. When you are in doubt, be still and know that I am God—not just any God, but *the* God, your God. I have the power to save. I have the power to redeem. I have the power to heal. I have the power to restore.

I will restore you. I will refresh you. I will empower you. I will feed you. I will nourish you. I will protect you. I will transform you. I will hold you always in my loving arms. You will never be the same again because you are always a new creation in me.

2 Corinthians 5:17
This means that anyone who belongs to Christ has become a new person. The old life is gone; a new life has begun!

30. Go Forth and Sing a New Song

You are a fragrant aroma to my heart. Your whispers of love directed toward my heart fill my throne room with such a sweet and pleasing fragrance. Stand strong today! Be brave and courageous!

In the midst of trials and tribulations come many victories, big and small. I am with you to guide you and direct your every step as you call upon my name and seek direction for your life. Your obedience to follow my Word and stand on my precepts will go far in my kingdom.

Let my light of love shine within you at all times. Go forth and sing a new song unto your King who is proud to call you Friend.

Psalm 98:1
Sing a new song to the Lord, for he has done
wonderful deeds. His right hand has won a mighty
victory; his holy arm has shown his saving power!

31. *You Are Wrapped in My Loving Arms*

*A*ll you need to do is reach out to me and I will take you by the hand and lead you beside still waters. Be encouraged and know this—you are wrapped in my loving arms and I will never let you go.

Take a step out of the boat and walk with me upon the waters. Do not be afraid for as I speak peace over your life there will be peace.

Why is it that the journey seems so long and arduous, you ask? The pathway to living in the fullness of my presence is narrow. It is my job to help refine you and present you before my Father as holy and blameless.

Isaiah 40:11
He will feed his flock like a shepherd. He will carry
the lambs in his arms, holding them close to his heart.
He will gently lead the mother sheep with their young.

32. I Am Pleased with You

Beloved Child, you radiate today with my Spirit of joy within you. I will shine a light into the darkness to bring you the fullness of my light. Just as a shepherd keeps his sheep, you will find the lost and brokenhearted and speak to their hearts with love and compassion.

Never have I been so proud to call you my Beloved Child. You are radiant and stand out among many brethren. I see a great light in you that burns brightly from dawn to dusk. When I call upon your name, your heart is turned toward me. You hear my voice and heed my wisdom when I speak softly and gently to you.

This life of yours is nothing in comparison to the eternal glory you will experience when I call you home. You have laid your life down for me. Oh, that you could see what I have in store for you! You shall not be disappointed. You shall rejoice. You will wake up each day with a new fervor to serve your Master and King.

My Child of Grace—I love you. I am pleased with your sacrificial life of giving to others without expecting anything in return—doing it all out of obedience to your Lord and Savior. Nothing you do or say or think goes unnoticed by me.

Beloved Child, there is a song in your heart. Sing it forth and believe it! The song pouring forth from your heart is my song to you.

I will meet all of your needs. Yes, I will meet all of your needs.

Exodus 33:13
If it is true that you look favorably on me, let me know your ways so I may understand you more fully and continue to enjoy your favor. And remember that this nation is your very own people.

33. I Will Be There to Help and Guide You

Beloved Child of my heart, I am with you to the end. I am in the midst of all your circumstances. I am a shield about you. Never once do I slumber when it comes to looking after you. I keep a watchful eye upon you at all times.

Think of a storm. I stand in the eye of the storm, the peaceful center, that place where you can be with me in the midst of the storm as you give all your anxieties to me. I am the peacemaker. I go ahead of you on your behalf and clear any pathway that may be obstructing your advancement in my kingdom.

Let me take you by the hand and lead you up a new path to the mountain top, to a new level where I can speak to you in those quiet places where you rest with me. Upon the mountain you shall see things at a new vantage point. At times the winds blow and the clouds sweep in so that as you are scaling the mountain, you can no longer see the mountain top.

It is in those times you need to put all your trust in me; for as you do, I will take position in your life as your mountain guide. You do not have to see the end from the beginning to continue upward on your journey. I am always there right beside you.

At times you will feel confident enough to climb and move forward on your own as you walk in my wisdom. At other times, you will need to hold my hand. Wherever you are on your journey, I will be there to help and guide you. I am calling you to the mountain top where you will be able to see things the way I see things and receive new wisdom, insight, and understanding.

Come forth! Be courageous! Be encouraged! Come and follow me and I shall give you rest.

Psalm 139:10
Even there your hand will guide me, and your
strength will support me.

34. I Love You Beyond Compare

*D*earest Child, I love you beyond compare. Stand strong amidst the storms of life. You will prevail for I am with you. Be strong today and remember I am with you. When you feel lost, call upon my name. When you feel afraid, come and hide in my arms. When you feel bewildered, seek my Word. My truth shall make a way for you always—the way of righteousness.

Psalm 36:7
How precious is your unfailing love, O God! All humanity finds shelter in the shadow of your wings.

35. *I Will Give You Rest as You Call Upon My Name*

My Child, lift up your eyes to your Maker and know that I am God. I will always be with you in your time of need. I am your comforter and protector. As the storms of life rage, I am the one who calms the storm. Release your fears and take my hand. You need not worry for I am here to take care of you.

As you sleep, angels are singing my praises in your presence so that you are drawn into the heavens in your spirit. As you awake, I set my angels about you to guard and protect you.

There is a song in the heavens with your name on it—it is the song of your heart that cries out to me, "Lord God, help me! I love you and I need you now more than ever." I hear your cries, the love song of your heart, and my heart is turned with compassion toward you.

Let me soothe you with my tenderness toward you. Receive my grace and mercy, the glimpses of joy that spark in your heart even amidst the storm. Hold on to the little tender mercies I send your way, for they shall give you the strength you need to make it through each day.

I am the Healer. Healing that takes place starts within the heart first. Even in sickness, your heart can grow stronger and your praises sing louder.

Take this time of adversity and rest completely in me. I will give you rest as you call upon my name. Sweet songs of love are pouring over you—sweet songs of joy are coming your way. Sweet songs of love I sing to you every day.

I am with you every moment. You are never alone.

Matthew 11:28
Then Jesus said, "Come to me, all of you who are weary and carry heavy burdens, and I will give you rest."

36. *Hold On to the Hope I Have Given You*

Sweet Child, how I long to have you sit in my presence and soak in my majesty. You are wonderful in the sight of your Maker. You have made tremendous strides in your journey to my heart. You are an overcomer. With me you are victorious. Your life shall bring glory to my name.

I care for all your needs, big and small. I am your protector. I am your great provider. No one shall thwart the plans I have for your life for I have called you by name. You are mine. You are chosen. You belong to the Almighty One.

Songs of deliverance and freedom are flowing down from the heavens above to rest upon your heart this day. Receive this music as a sweet comfort to your heart. Joy in great measure I am giving to you, my Child. Righteousness and truth are presiding over your heart and mind. Wisdom into the things that are incomprehensible will give you new insight and revelation.

Listen to that still, small voice within your heart that tells you which way to turn at every crossroad in your life. Pour out your heart to those who come running to you longing to know me. I will show you how much love I hold in my heart for all my dear ones.

I want to bless you for your faithfulness and trust in me. Receive all that I send you in the way of love and comfort from those I place in your midst.

You do not always have to be strong. Let me be strong for you. Your strength in me will in turn give you the rest you desire. The peace that you long for will envelop your heart and soul every day as you rest in me.

Bring all your concerns to me and I will break every area of bondage and every stronghold that tries to get in the way of the blessed life that I hold in my hand just for you. I am your Mighty Savior, and you are my precious child of resiliency. Hold on to the hope I have given you; it shall never disappoint.

Psalm 71:14
But I will keep on hoping for your help;
I will praise you more and more.

37. You Can Confidently Trust That I Am Always There

*D*earest Child, I am with you and I am in you. Your heart is aligned to mine. In seeking my face you will come to know deeper truths into the mysteries of my ways. I am the way, the truth, and the life. All that I have I give to you in abundance.

Quietly come before me and share your deepest thoughts. I will meet you there always. Although you may not always hear me or feel me, you can confidently trust that I am always there. I will never leave you nor forsake you.

I know the concerns that weigh upon your heart. I have heard the cries of your heart and know the things which are holding you down. Come to me and I will lift your burdens and realign your thoughts with mine. I will give you wisdom that will lead you to truth that brings freedom.

You are free in me, my Child. I will keep you with me always. In your darkest moments you are never alone. Rest in me and enjoy your day. I will bring new things your way that will bring a smile to your face.

Matthew 28:19-20
Therefore, go and make disciples of all the nations, baptizing them in the name of the Father and the Son and the Holy Spirit. Teach these new disciples to obey all the commands I have given you. And be sure of this: I am with you always, even to the end of the age.

38. I Will Continue to Reveal Myself to You

*D*earest Child, you are Beloved of My Heart. Today I stand at the door of your heart and knock. It is a new day to revel in the goodness I have surrounded you with. Take the time today to reflect on all that I am doing in your life, on all the blessings big and small.

It is with great joy that I look upon you. I have filled you with love and compassion. I am a shield about you. I am your everlasting joy. I am the one who takes you by the hand and leads the inspirations of your heart. I bring you into a new place with me each and every day.

Yes, your days will hold challenges, but that is why I am here for you to lean on. What pleases my heart is your honesty in revealing your heart and thoughts to me. You share it all. The more honest you are with me, the more honest you are becoming with yourself. That is how you grow and mature in your faith.

Continue to reveal yourself to me and I will continue to reveal myself to you. I do not withhold my love from you. My love is constant. I am your constant companion.

Isaiah 52:6
But I will reveal my name to my people, and they will come to know its power. Then at last they will recognize that I am the one who speaks to them.

39. My Word Is Your Armor

S weet and tender heart, you are delicate yet strong. The fire of my love burns within you shedding new light and life to those I place around you. When your heart is feeling fragile, I will be the packaging that keeps you from breaking. I will provide layers of protection over your heart and mind.

My very Word is your strength, your armor. Remember who you are in me. Remember all the promises I speak of in my Word. Call forth things that are not as though they are in accord with my Word. My Word is your truth. My Word is your covering. My Word is life.

Be not weary when the enemy strategizes against you, using your very friends to cause you woe. The enemy is always going to try to hit you where it hurts the most.

Friendships can bring strength and friendships can bring you down when hearts are not aligned to my will. Remember that I am your greatest and truest friend and I will never let you down.

When you listen to my counsel you will rise above the pettiness and walk in peace. I am your peace. I am your resting place.

Rest in me. No matter how hard the enemy hits you, even in your blind spots, I will be the truth that sets you free. Do for others as you would want them to do for you. In doing this, my peace will rest upon you.

Ephesians 6:13-17
Therefore, put on every piece of God's armor so you
will be able to resist the enemy in the time of evil.
Then after the battle you will still be standing firm.
Stand your ground, putting on the belt of truth and
the body armor of God's righteousness. For shoes, put
on the peace that comes from the Good News so that

you will be fully prepared. In addition to all of these, hold up the shield of faith to stop the fiery arrows of the devil. Put on salvation as your helmet, and take the sword of the Spirit, which is the word of God.

40. *I Am All the Strength You Need*

I want you to know that whenever the task before you seems too daunting, it is before you for a reason. I want to show you how strong you have become. You may think you are weak, but you are indeed strong for I am within you and I am strong. I am all the strength you need.

Call upon my name within your heart and mind and I will come running to you. Whenever the day looks bleak and the rain is pouring down, know that I am here to bring rays of sunshine into your heart. Even on the grayest of days, my light is shining—the light that warms your heart and refreshes your spirit.

Philippians 4:13
For I can do everything through Christ, who gives me strength.

41. There Is Nothing That Is Too Big for Me

*T*here is nothing that is too big for me. There is nothing that is too difficult for me. There is nothing that will get in the way of my plans for your life as long as you continue to seek my face. I will be with you every step of the way.

Jeremiah 32:17
O Sovereign Lord! You made the heavens and earth
by your strong hand and powerful arm. Nothing is too
hard for you!

42. I Became Nothing so You Could Become Something

Today is a new day. As you have walked through the fire with me, so too shall you walk in the light of the sun with me—clear skies, warm breezes, birds singing.

When you have doubt, come to me into my chamber where we can converse. I will share with you the secrets of my kingdom, words of wisdom that will bring you insight into how to live your life to the fullest day by day.

My sacrifice was for you. I gave myself for you. I became nothing so you could become something. And as I rose, so shall you. You shall prosper in many new ways, ways unthought-of of by you.

I will lead you gently. You will sail with me, my Spirit moving you in the direction you should go. Step aside and let me go before you. Let me clear the pathways for you.

If you are always asking, you shall receive. If you are always seeking, you shall find. If you are always knocking, I will open doors for you that you never knew could be opened and oftentimes never even knew were there.

Remember, my love for you is abundant and limitless. You have come so far and have so much further to go. This new journey will take you where you never thought you could go. I will show you how much I love you. You will see it in the abundant fruit that is ready for harvest in your life.

This is your time. This is your place. This is your new life. Are you ready? Come and follow me.

2 Timothy 2:11
This is a trustworthy saying: If we die with him, we will also live with him.

43. My Word Alone Will Break through Walls

Beloved of My Heart, you are shining like a diamond in my kingdom. Your prayers resonate in the heavens and are gathered unto my heart. As I look upon you, my heart smiles for I am proud of you. I am proud of the way you so earnestly cry out to me and reverently give me praise and honor.

Be of good cheer for your Savior is with you to the very end and beyond. I am with you always.

As you come up against a wall, take my Word and proclaim its truths. My Word alone will break through walls. My Words uttered through the lips of my righteous and obedient servants have a cascading effect in this world—they reach abroad, far and wide.

I am bringing you to a new level, a higher level, a place where I will share with you new and intimate truths about who I am and who you are to me. I am proud of you. I am with you. I love you.

John 17:17
Make them holy by your truth; teach them your word, which is truth.

44. I Am the One Who Carries You through the Storm

I am the one who carries you through the storm. I am the one that picks you up where you have fallen, holds you, comforts you, restores your confidence and sends you on your way again—this time with a better plan for a more fulfilling journey.

When you get stuck in a snare set by the enemy, know this—you are never stuck, for I am Lord of all. As you abandon your own will and submit to me, my Spirit is able to penetrate your heart at a deeper level. That is when I unravel thoughts that have collided with fear of the unknown.

Remember, I know all and scc where you have been, where you are, and where you are heading. If I see that you are leaning in the wrong direction, as a loving parent I have many ways of leading you back to the path I have set before you. Sometimes it is through discipline, which can be painful, but not the kind of pain that disables—the kind of pain that enables and causes you to grown and learn.

Be encouraged, for I am with you and for you.

Luke 8:24
The disciples went and woke him up, shouting,
"Master, Master, we're going to drown!" When Jesus
woke up, he rebuked the wind and the raging waves.
Suddenly the storm stopped and all was calm.

45. Set Aside Some Time This Day to Draw Near Me

*D*earest Child, you are a joy to my heart. I am thrilled when you experience the kind of joy that comes from me, for it is the truest form of joy. As you revel in all that I am doing in your life, your heart shall be uplifted for you shall see that I am God and I do follow through with my promises spoken of in my Word—at all times, in every occasion.

My truth is everlasting. My promises are for you—to guide you, to lead you down uncharted territories within your heart.

My Dear Child, you must know that as your loving Father, I want the very best for you. What I have to offer has no limits for I am limitless. Things that may seem impossible or improbable to you are possible through me and in me.

Set aside some time this day to draw near to me—a moment of stillness where your thoughts rest in me and I will speak to you. In this quiet moment, I will refresh you and let you know that I am with you and I am proud of you.

Thank you for taking the time to be with me; it is my greatest pleasure. Where your treasure is, there will be your heart. You are my treasure and my heart is with you always!

Hebrews 10:22
Let us go right into the presence of God with sincere hearts fully trusting him. For our guilty consciences have been sprinkled with Christ's blood to make us clean, and our bodies have been washed with pure water.

46. *I Am Building a New Strength of Character within You*

My loving, precious Child, I know that you are seeking comfort and hope in areas that have brought you dismay and discord. Help is on the way, dear one. I am here to stand by your side and stand strong on your behalf.

When you sink into the depths of despair you are never alone, though it may seem as though you are. In the darkness I will shine a light. In the darkness, I will penetrate those areas that need healing with the salve from heaven that my Father used to bind up my wounds.

Remember that before I was brought into the house of my Father, I was plunged into the pits of hell, all so I could rise up and defeat the world's enemy. The enemy would love (if it were possible for him to love) for you to fall into the pits of darkness and keep you there bound up. But that is impossible, for I will never let my children go, and you are my most beloved child.

As you have followed after me, you have been persecuted for my name's sake and have followed in my footsteps. My footsteps take you on the narrow path, but this path leads to life.

You are in the process of completely dying to yourself so that you may rise completely to a new life in me. As the parts of you that you have held on to for so many years are being unbound by me, your wounds are being exposed. These wounds need exposure to my light in order to heal properly. If they are kept bound up you will not be able to realize the specific areas that need to be exposed to my light.

The deeper you fall, the higher you will rise up. I would have it that you rise up to the very top, so that you have entrance into a special sanctuary in my Father's house that is set apart for those who have persevered.

I am building a new strength of character within you. All battles come to an end, my Dearest Child. The one you are currently in is drawing near its end, and I have sent my warrior angels to guard and protect you so that you do not stumble.

Be brave, my Child. Be courageous. Be still before me. Always remember that I am God.

Isaiah 12:2
See, God has come to save me. I will trust in him and not be afraid. The Lord God is my strength and my song; he has given me victory.

47. I Forgive You

*D*earest Child, do you know that you are forgiven completely when you come to me asking for forgiveness? Do you really believe that you are? I have washed you as white as snow. I have cleaned the slate so that you may begin again fresh and renewed.

Why do I forgive you? The answer is simple—because I love you. I created you to be who you are this day.

As you walk through your days with everything that a day holds, you are bound to fall because you are human. But you are destined to rise up again as I have first risen for you.

Do not be ashamed to come to me for there is nothing to hide. I already know what you are going through in your thoughts, your actions, and in your heart. By coming to me for mercy and acceptance, you will find that I am indeed merciful and fully accept you in every way.

Baring your heart and acknowledging your sin before me opens up a window in your heart where the sin flows out and a renewed spirit flows in. Sometimes it is difficult to face your own sin but you do not have to do it alone. I am always here as your friend ready to listen and receive, wash, and redeem.

Do I forgive you? Yes. I always will as you seek my face and turn your heart toward righteousness. Be confident in this truth. I forgive you.

Psalm 32:5
Finally, I confessed all my sins to you and stopped trying to hide my guilt. I said to myself, "I will confess my rebellion to the Lord." And you forgave me! All my guilt is gone.

48. *My Love for You Is Constant*

I want you to know that I love you. I want you to know that I am proud of you. I want you to know that I consider you worthy— worthy of all my love, of all I have to give my precious children.

You are my precious child. When you lack confidence in who I created you to be, come to me in my Word and I will shower you with my promises and my loving kindness. When you feel void of my presence, lift up your heart to mine and I will embrace you with arms wide open. I will show you in many different ways how much I love you and how you are such a treasure to my heart.

Be encouraged and know that I am leading you down the right path. There is so much joy that I am sending your way—joy that will break down any walls that have come between our hearts. Once those walls come down, and they will, you will see my divinity in a different light.

You will receive clarity in the realm of my spirit that draws you into the shelter of the Most High. In this place of shelter, I will pour over you life-giving words of love, grace, and mercy. In this place you will know how much I love you.

My love for you is constant—it remains the same no matter where you are in life. I never leave your side. Remember and know that I want the very best for your life. I see what your heart is striving after and I am here to take you to that next level.

Exceeding joy is awaiting you. You are joy to my heart just as you are today! Come away with me in your heart! I am waiting for you.

Psalm 103:17
But the love of the Lord remains forever with those
who fear him. His salvation extends to the children's
children.

49. *You Are the Apple of My Eye*

You will see all around you that there are people who need to hear an encouraging word. My children want to feel special. You are special to me and that is what matters the most. You are the apple of my eye.

It does not matter what other people think about you. What matters is what I think about you. I want you to know this day that I think the world of you just this very moment. I am proud of you. I cherish you.

Psalm 17:8
Guard me as you would guard your own eyes. Hide
me in the shadow of your wings.

50. I Have Gone Before You to Make Your Path Straight

*T*oday as you set about your journey, remember to give all your thoughts and cares to me. I will show you the way to go. At every turn my hand is there to guide you. I have gone before you to make your path straight.

Proverbs 4:11
I will teach you wisdom's ways and lead you in straight paths.

51. I Am Walking Right by Your Side

*D*earest One, my heart goes out to you this day. In these moments of sadness, loneliness, and despair, know this—I will never let you go. You are precious to my eyes. Just as you have laid your heart bare before me, I open up my heart completely to you.

Rest in the comfort of my heart which is steadfast and true. I will make a way for you in the desert. I will lead you down the path that will bring you renewed strength, life, and hope. I want you to know that your best years are yet to come. Continue to hold tight to me.

Delight in me and I will give you the desires of your heart. You have walked a lonely road at times, but I have always walked down that road with you even when you were not aware that I was there. It is that way this day. I am walking right by your side.

Be comforted. I delight in you. All will be well.

Psalm 23:4
Even when I walk through the darkest valley, I will
not be afraid, for you are close beside me. Your rod
and your staff protect and comfort me.

52. Let Go of the Burdens You Are Carrying

O h Tender Heart, do not be dismayed for I am your God. Yes, I will strengthen you and help you and hold you close as you walk down this burdensome path. This day will break forth to a new day. A new day is a new opportunity to make the best of even the most difficult circumstances. I am right by your side.

Let go of all the burdens you are carrying. Give it all to me. Allow me to lighten your load. I am here for you. I am as close to you as you are to yourself. I am in your heart and know that you are longing for comfort. Be not weary. Be not sad. I want you to know that no matter what you are going through, I have come so that you may find rest.

Allow the rivers of my living water to cleanse your heart and renew your mind. I am doing a great work within your heart even amidst your pain.

Not one tear goes unnoticed by me. Not one sigh is unheard by me. Not one cry escapes my ears. I hear you. I love you. I know what you need and I am here this day to bring you one step closer to my heart. I have come so that you may find joy again. It is coming. This I promise you.

Matthew 11:30
For my yoke is easy to bear, and the burden I give you is light.

53. Draw Near to Me

*D*earest Child, I am with you now even to the end of the ages. Surrounding you are choirs of angels singing praises along with you unto me in the heavens. In your moments of worship and praise, I am in your midst in a special way.

I minister to your heart as you pour out your heart and soul in song to your Maker. I am the one who brings good tidings, and I am here to tell you that you are a winner.

You have risen to the next level and I am ready to show you who I am and what I am all about. I am in your heart whispering your name. Draw near to me, for within my heart is a treasure for you to behold.

I give unto you my heart! Rejoice, for a new day is dawning and within this day I will bless you in many ways. Believe in the power of my transforming love and you will see me work wonders in your life.

Be at peace this day, for I am right by your side.

Psalm 73:28
But as for me, how good it is to be near God!
I have made the Sovereign Lord my shelter,
and I will tell everyone about the wonderful things
you do.

54. Hope in Victory

*A*s you call upon my name I come running to you. I hear your every thought. Your heart's cry reaches the throne room of my Father. Yes, my Child, this is a battle you are in, but do not fear for I am your captain and it is my responsibility to lead you safely to shore.

The waters rage about you, but there is still within you the peace that comes from me. As you slip into the dark waters, I will rescue you. I have come with many so that you will not drown.

Your victory is bigger than yourself. Your victory will empower you to help others that have fallen into the same deep waters. That hope in me is your hope in victory. It is that very hope that makes me proud of you. It is that very hope within you that draws me to you.

Hope is light, my Child. Your hope in me is drawing in my light. Your hope in me is reaching the heavens. I have charged my greatest angels to surround and protect you so that you do not stumble.

1 Corinthians 15:57
***But thank God! He gives us victory over sin and death
through our Lord Jesus Christ.***

55. I Am Carrying You Through

*I*n the midst of your trials I will come along beside you and carry you through. You do not have to carry your burdens alone. Allow me to lift them from your shoulders and bring you to a new place with me.

I am the one who will never leave your side. I am the one who will show you the way to go. I am the one who will never disappoint you.

I know you have been disappointed many times in your life by others. You have also experienced the effects of what you may see as failures. You are not a failure. You are an overcomer. You keep on going even despite the circumstances you are facing.

How is it that you are able to make it through these rough times? I am carrying you through. I am breathing my breath of hope within you. You may not even realize that it is I who is moving within you to make it through the day.

I want for you to know that even when my children do not come to me, I still move on their behalf. You do not have to come to me for me to be with you for I am always with you. It is the desire of my heart that you come to me because I want to teach you new things about yourself and your life that will help you grow and mature in your faith.

Draw near to me this day and I will draw near to you. Be content in the little things. Be thankful for the blessings I send your way. I send you my blessings just because I love you and want you to taste and see my goodness. I look forward to every moment you call upon my name.

Go now and walk into this new day with fervor to be a light unto my children and to brighten someone's day. I will give you what you need always.

Psalm 63:8
***I cling to you; your strong right hand holds me
securely.***

56. Not One Thought or Cry Escapes from My Ears

*L*et your heart be glad this day, for I am here to bring you good tidings—to spread the word to all my children and let you know that I love you beyond compare. There is nothing that is insignificant to me; not one thought or cry from your heart escapes from my ears.

I capture all your tears in my hand and release a refreshing rain upon your spirit to bring you comfort. So many times you have cried out to me and have felt that I have not answered you. Oh, my Child, I always answer, but my ways are mysterious to you just as my love for you is fathomless. My love will never escape you.

It may feel as though I have abandoned you at times or failed to answer your prayers. Please trust that my infinite love is doing a great work in you during these times. The effects of my love are ever reaching to the ends of time and beyond. This is your opportunity to take my hand and walk with me.

In your desperate moments, simply trust in me and I will show you the way to my heart. You will never be lost for I am always at your side. I come to rescue you from where you have fallen. I come to lift you up and dust you off and put you back on the right path, the path of righteousness.

I am doing a new work in you this day. Reach out to me, take my hand and walk with me. I have much to share with you.

Psalm 22:24
For he has not ignored or belittled the suffering of the needy. He has not turned his back on them, but has listened to their cries for help.

57. I Will Bring You Encouragement

S eeker of My Heart, come to me so that you may find rest. In moments of quiet with me, you will come to know me in deeper, more intimate ways. I have much to share with you. I want you to rest in the comfort of my loving presence.

Let me lift the burden off of your shoulders. Allow my healing rains to wash you, cleanse you, and free you from all of your anxieties.

When you are discouraged, come to me and I will bring you encouragement. When you are exhausted, come to me and I will bring you rest. When you are joyful, come to me and we can rejoice together in all the greatness of my love that pours over you day and night.

Not one moment passes when I am not with you. I know what you are going through this day and I am here to let you know that despite the trials, you will be victorious for your King and Savior has gone to battle for you.

When you are weak, I am strong. Do not be dismayed for I am with you. Lift up your eyes to me and believe that I love you beyond compare. As you pour out your heart to me, I open the floodgates of heaven upon your life to bring you the peace that passes all understanding.

Be of good cheer for it is a new day, a day of blessings for you and for all of my beloved children who are calling upon my name.

James 4:10
Humble yourselves before the Lord, and he will lift
you up in honor.

58. I Will Bring You Comfort

My sweet child, I am with you. I travel right by your side everywhere you go. I never leave your side. I send my guardian angels to watch over you day and night.

Release all your fears to me and I will bring you comfort. My peace rests upon you this hour. I want for you to remember that you are never outside of my love.

Psalm 119:76
Now let your unfailing love comfort me, just as you promised me, your servant.

59. I Have Come to Fill You with Joy

*I*n the darkness of the world that is filled with angry, hurting people—my light is within you to bring joy to others. At times you may feel as though there is no joy in your heart. That is alright, for I have come to fill you with joy as you walk with me. Your joy can come through the simple gift of hope I give to you this day.

Keep hope alive within your heart. Remember to think on good things. I am good and my goodness is for you and in you.

Psalm 19:8
The commandments of the Lord are right, bringing
joy to the heart. The commands of the Lord are clear,
giving insight for living.

60. *You Are Wonderful to Me*

I am making a way for you in this world. I go before you to make your path straight. As you journey down the trail of life, remember that you are not walking alone. Sometimes you may feel alone. Sometimes you may feel as though you have lost your way. You are not lost because you are not alone—I am with you. I have the directions with me that will lead you to a better place.

Stand up and proclaim the truth of my Word, and in doing so you will be opening doors that may have been locked to you in the past. I have the keys.

Come home, my Beloved—come and sit at my banquet table and let me share with you how much I love you. Let me pour over you life-giving words of encouragement and hope to brighten your day.

I don't think you realize how wonderful you are to me. You have been made wonderful by your Creator, out of my undying love for you. Take some time this day to reflect on my goodness—to reflect on my majesty, to reflect on the greatness of your God—your God who sent his very own beloved Son to die for you, to wash away your sins and to raise you up to a new life with me.

Enjoy your day and know that you are the work of my hand and are my priceless masterpiece. I have called you today to be with me. I await your arrival and am here to tell you—I love you.

Psalm 139:14
Thank you for making me so wonderfully complex!
Your workmanship is marvelous—how well I know it.

61. I Have Heard the Cry of Your Heart

*P*recious Child, I want you to lift up your heart to me in prayer tonight. I have much to share with you. The road you have traveled has been long and arduous, but rest assured it has been worth the fight to receive the prize for which you have battled.

Your suffering has brought you to your knees before me countless times. I have heard every cry of your heart. I have captured every whisper of love you have poured out of your heart and soul to me. Your love of me has been your transformational grace that is molding you into the person I created you to be.

Come, my Child, to the banquet table and feast with me, your beloved Savior. I will shower you now with love that you have never received before—new love that is coming from my throne room in heaven. Savor every moment we share with one another.

You belong to me, Precious Heart. I will take good care of you always. I am overflowing with love for you. I am well pleased with you. Take my hand and walk with me. I will never let you down.

Psalm 18:6
But in my distress I cried out to the Lord; yes, I prayed to my God for help. He heard me from his sanctuary; my cry to him reached his ears.

62. It Is for My Glory

*I*t is for my glory that you have risen to new life. It is for my glory that you are victorious. It is for my glory that your testimony will bring hope to my children who are calling out to me.

You have been set free, my Child. This is your new season. This is the season of the great harvest. You will now reap what you have sown. You have sown your love in me and in return I will give unto you one hundredfold.

You cannot even imagine what I have in store for your life. You will no longer remain stagnant. You will now soar to new heights on eagles' wings. My winds of righteousness will carry you to places you have never been. Your years of hardship will be a distant memory to you. You have much to look forward to.

Continue spending time with me and I will pour out upon you great wisdom, understanding, and knowledge. A new day for you to shine like never before has arrived just in time for my glory to be revealed in you and through you.

Go forth and enjoy this new season. Rejoice in me as I rejoice in you. It is your day to shine. You are shining for my glory, which is upon you now and forever more!

Luke 2:14
Glory to God in highest heaven, and peace on earth to those with whom God is pleased.

63. I Am with You

O h, Lovely Child, I want for you to know that no matter what you do or where you go, I am with you. I have not forgotten you. I hold you near to my heart at all times.

This day remember to reflect on my goodness. Think of all the things I have done for you. In doing this, you will be strengthened in your spirit.

Perseverance is part of the journey to freedom. Keep on persevering and you will find the freedom you have been longing for.

Know this, my Child, I have called you to be a warrior—to lead the way, to break through walls and be victorious. Draw your strength from my life-giving Word. In my Word you will find all that you need to make it through your day successfully.

Be quiet before me and remember that I am God.

Isaiah 41:10
Don't be afraid, for I am with you. Don't be discouraged, for I am your God. I will strengthen you and help you. I will hold you up with my victorious right hand.

64. I Am Your Father Who Loves You

Oh sweet and tender Child of mine, how I love you. You are radiant and precious to me. I listen intently to your every prayer. I implore you to keep on seeking and you will find the answers deep within your heart where I reside.

Thank you for inviting me in to dwell with you. Thank you for making your heart my home. Even when you do things you are not happy about, I still love you. I understand you and want to teach you the right way—my way.

Do not worry anymore about the mistakes and failures of your past. Look forward to the future and remember to always keep your eyes steadfast upon me. I am your Father who loves you and wants the very best for you.

Take my hand and walk with me. See! I have much to give to you. As the desires of your heart align with my will, they will come to pass in the right time.

Be patient. Be still before me and be comforted in my presence. I place a mantle of protection upon you this night. It will never leave you for I am that mantle just as I am your covering.

Rest this night in my love. All will be well. Tomorrow is a new beginning for you. I give you a new day as my gift to you. Treasure me as I treasure you. Love me as I love you.

1 John 3:1
See how very much our Father loves us, for he calls
us his children, and that is what we are! But the
people who belong to this world don't recognize that
we are God's children because they don't know him.

65. I Am Intently Listening

I am intently listening to every word that you are sharing with me. I understand what you are working through in your heart and I am here to help you. When you are weary, come to me so that you can rest. You do not have to figure everything out in one night. Take it piece by piece, step by step. I am accompanying you on this journey so that you do not have to walk it alone.

Ask me anything. Tell me everything that is on your heart. Do not fear that I will reject you. I know everything there is to know about you and I love you completely just as you are this moment, imperfections and all. I want you to share it all so that we can sort out your thoughts together and bring them into alignment with my will for your life.

There is so much goodness for you to behold in your today and in your tomorrows. There is so much in store for you coming from me out of the treasuries of heaven. I want to show you my love in ways you have yet to experience.

Talk to me, my Child. I am listening.

Psalm 17:6
I am praying to you because I know you will answer, O God. Bend down and listen as I pray.

66. A Thankful Heart Brings Me Great Joy

*D*earest Child, do not fear, for I am holding on to you this day. Bring all your cares to me and I will shower you with my loving kindness. Continue pressing into me and I will continue to impart my wisdom and truth to you. You will come to understand all that I am doing in your life.

Everything has a purpose. All that you go through serves a perfect purpose. It may not seem perfect as you are going through it, but it is all part of the journey I laid out in front of you before you were even born. You are making your way through life like a champion. You keep on rising every time you fall. That is the champion spirit I placed within you.

Yes, it may seem like I have forsaken you at times. That is far from the truth. As life events unfold, you will be able to look back and see how I have woven your life together as part of a beautiful love song that has no end.

Your life is a love song. Sing to me within your heart this day and I will sing back to you. I give you all that I have. I have everything to give and I give it all to you. A thankful heart brings me great joy.

Today as your heart looks up to me—let your heart open up and smile. I have placed a smile in your heart. My Beloved, you make my heart smile!

Psalm 9:1
I will praise you, Lord, with all my heart; I will tell of
all the marvelous things you have done.

67. *Trust in Me*

My Child, I hear the cries of your heart. I know and understand your pain. I am here to wipe the tears that stream down your face as you look to me for answers.

There is nothing that is too difficult for me. It may seem too difficult for you but you are not alone. You do not have to carry the load alone. Allow me to lift the weight from your shoulders and strengthen your spirit.

Have hope, my child. Have hope. Trust in me and I will continue to keep that hope alive within you. That hope will give you the strength and courage to face the storm and walk through it with confidence. I am taking you by the hand this day and leading you to walk beside still waters.

Soak in my love for I give it to you in abundance. I am teaching you many things about yourself on this journey. What I teach you will help you discern the direction you need to take.

You are doing well. You may not feel that way but I want you to feel assured that you are indeed doing well simply because you are reaching out to me.

In the midst of your circumstances remember to be thankful and that will help you to change your mindset and help keep you on the right course. Believe and hope. I am with you to satisfy the longings of your heart. Be patient, for they are coming just in time.

Isaiah 12:2
See, God has come to save me. I will trust in him and
not be afraid. The Lord God is my strength and my
song; he has given me victory.

68. I Am Your Strength When You Are Weak

*M*y Beloved Child, do not be dismayed for I am with you. I am your strong tower and your shield. I stand with you in the midst of your trials. I am teaching you how to trust me in deeper ways.

Your longings do not go unnoticed by me. I know all the desires of your heart, for it is I who placed them there to begin with.

I am cultivating your heart, mind, and soul to be a warrior who will stand in the gap for others who are hurting, lost, and broken. In the secret places of your heart where we meet each day, I am teaching you new things.

It may seem like one day floats into another with no changes. Realize that you are exercising your spiritual muscles every time you come to me exposing your hurts, trusting that I will lift you up to higher places.

Your faithfulness is making you stronger and stronger each day. You may not realize how strong you have become. You will recognize your strength in the days to come as you see the answers to your prayers for yourself and others spring to life before your very eyes.

Be encouraged and rest in me. Remember this—I am your strength when you are weak.

Isaiah 40:29
He gives power to the weak and strength to the powerless.

69. I Am About to Do a New Thing

My love surrounds you. My compassion carries you through the most difficult days. Be encouraged for I am about to do a new thing in your life—something unexpected. The tides do change and so do life circumstances. From deep within your heart I will raise up a new, vibrant, and healthy crop of righteousness. The great harvest is at hand, so prepare yourself this hour and follow after me.

Be kind to those who are good to you and to those who cause you woe. My children who are hurting need a kind word to bring light and hope to their day. Oftentimes those who do not know me are those who are hurting the most. The hurt that they may bring you is a manifestation of the hurt and emptiness they feel inside.

I will give you the grace to show my love to these souls as I call my lost sheep into my fold. Be patient and above all—love.

Isaiah 42:9
Everything I prophesied has come true, and now I
will prophesy again. I will tell you the future before it
happens.

70. I Do Have a Plan for You

S eek me with all of your heart. Draw near to me and I will draw near to you. Believe in me. Believe that I honor your prayers and answer them in love.

Sometimes you are faced with adversity and trials that seem too difficult to bear. I understand the trial you are going through. I am here to help you weather this storm.

No matter how hard the wind is blowing or how turbulent the waters are rushing about you—I am with you holding you tighter than you can imagine and I will never let you go. Please do not let go of me.

This storm will pass even as the pain may linger. You cannot see the end from the beginning as I do. You can only press forward each day and hold on to my promise that I will never leave you nor forsake you even in this dark hour. I do have a plan for you though it may not be clear to you now.

I will send many your way to gird you up and speak hope into your life. Hope against all hope and I will make a way for you and your family. I have each one of you in the palm of my hand. I am the comfort you need and I give it to you this day in abundance. You have sought after me in this storm and have been faithful to trust in me despite the circumstances you are facing. I will make a way where there seems to be no way.

There is beauty that will rise out of the ashes through it all and you will know that I am your God. I look upon you this day with great compassion.

Jeremiah 29:11
"For I know the plans I have for you," says the Lord.
"They are plans for good and not for disaster, to give you a future and a hope."

71. I Am Preparing You

*W*alk in my light this day. As you embark upon a new journey, take my hand and let me lead you beside still waters. I look upon you with great admiration for your faithfulness and loyalty to my calling upon your life.

Be encouraged and realize that not one prayer or thought toward me goes unnoticed. I have called you to be a warrior in my kingdom, to fight the battle for goodness through prayer. I take your prayers and bring them before my Father, pleading on your behalf and on behalf of those you are praying for.

Many people in your life have brought you sorrows over the years, but be not dismayed for your faithfulness to me as you have guarded yourself from the attacks of the enemy will be counted to you as righteousness. Release those hurts to me and allow my spirit of forgiveness to cleanse your heart, soul, and mind so that you may walk before me in purity.

I am preparing you for the day when I take you before my Father. On that day you will fully realize my redemption and all that took place when I died on the cross for you.

You cannot turn back the hands of time, but you can make good and holy choices this day, this moment. Your sins are forgiven the moment you ask for forgiveness.

Do not allow the enemy to plague you with your past sins and failures. Move forward. It is indeed a new day to walk in righteousness. I will always help you along the way as you ask of me.

I go before you during your day and orchestrate things on your behalf. I am preparing you to become stronger in your faith as will be needed in the days ahead. You are called to be a light unto my children. My light in you shines hope upon the lives of others you come in contact with each day. You may not realize the impact you have in my kingdom for simply being you—the you I created you to be.

Trust in me that your faithfulness has a great reward. Walk in my light this day as I send you many blessings just because I love you.

John 14:3
When everything is ready, I will come and get you, so that you will always be with me where I am.

72. I Am Calling You to Step out of the Boat

My Child, I understand where you are right now. Trust that I am with you, even though you do not feel my presence. I am teaching you a new thing. I am calling you to step out of the boat and stand on the water with me. Do not be afraid for I am with you.

Even though you cannot see all that I am doing behind the scenes on your behalf—trust in me. Believe in me and all will be well with your soul. I love you beyond compare.

You are a treasure to be hidden no longer. I am here to bring you out into the world under the radiant glow of my light. My light is your covering and protection this day.

Matthew 14:29
"Yes, come," Jesus said. So Peter went over the side of the boat and walked on the water toward Jesus.

73. I Am Faithful to Answer

My Gracious Child, I am with you today. When you are in a place of dissatisfaction with your life, be quiet before me and remember that I am God.

I am speaking to you on many different levels. I am speaking to your heart, your mind, and your soul. As you are fervently seeking my direction for your life, remember that I am a God who is faithful to answer. I am listening intently to the cries of your heart.

When you are unsettled in your spirit that is a sign that there is a battle going on around you. If you are not able to see it with your eyes, then it is a battle that is being fought in the realm of the Spirit. Take my Word and fight the good fight and you will be victorious. As you seek answers, you will find them.

There will be days where you will need to just wait on me and be patient. Be patient, my Child, be patient. Sing a new song to me this day and I will capture it in my arms. I will pour out on you a new rain that will freshen the air and cleanse your spirit.

The sun is shining and the birds are singing. Join them as you praise my name and you will be filled with the fullness of my light!

Matthew 7:7
Keep on asking, and you will receive what you ask for.
Keep on seeking, and you will find. Keep on knocking,
and the door will be opened to you.

74. I Will Go before You and Make Your Path Straight

A new day has arrived! Come and take a walk with me! I will refresh your spirit and renew your mind. Before you set out on your day, turn your eyes toward me. I will help you to walk in truth and righteousness.

Be right! Do right! Live right! Purpose in your mind to brighten someone's day with a smile. Speak with confidence and enthusiasm as you walk in my joy.

Be grateful! Be thankful! Be hopeful! Be joyful! Be full of love! No matter how you are feeling when you begin your day, first acknowledge my presence and pray your day forward. I will go before you and make your path straight.

I am full of love for you!

Proverbs 3:6
***Seek his will in all you do, and he will show you which
path to take.***

75. You Were Born for This

My hand of victory is upon you. You are steeped in my love and overflowing with abundant grace. My majesty rests upon your shoulders to give you all the strength you need to fulfill my greatest purpose for your life.

You are coming in on the home stretch. Reach out and take my baton. Win the race and receive your prize that I have held in my hand just for you. All will see my glory. All glory and honor goes to the Father who has given you new life.

I am expanding your horizons and enlarging your territories. All deposits of your faith in me are being credited back to you in amazing proportions. Rise to the occasion and pursue your greatest dream. It is I who placed the dream in your heart.

You were born for this, in this time, this place, this day. Grace is being poured out upon you through my hands and the hands of our Father. Go now and claim your victory. It will be everlasting and true born out of perseverance, faith, and trust in me.

I am running with you, setting the pace by which you will have the energy to sprint to the finish line with great speed and agility. This marathon of life that has been a continuing challenge will break forth into a new season.

I am with you to refresh your spirit. I have equipped you with what you need to call my children to meet me at the finish line. All will see my glory and know that you belong to me, my Winning Child.

Exodus 9:16
But I have spared you for a purpose—to show you my
power and to spread my fame throughout the earth.

76. *This Battle Has Already Been Won!*

When you are downtrodden and struggling with despair and hopelessness, look up. Cast your cares upon me and allow me to be your protection.

When facing the giants in your life, come to me first and I will endow your spirit with the finest armory that will protect you from the fiery darts of the enemy. Satan is very crafty and skilled at twisting around your own thoughts, steeping them with negativity and making it seem as though those thoughts are coming from yourself. This is why it is so important for you to call upon my name.

My Spirit will make my Word come alive within you so that you can slay those thoughts and put them to rest by replacing them with the truth. The truth is that you were fearfully and wonderfully made. The truth is that no weapon formed against you will prevail. The truth is that my love for you never fails.

Even if you feel as if you are alone in this battle, remember this truth—I will never leave you nor forsake you. My truth will send the enemy to flight and set you free. The enemy has no power to stand up against the truth, and as you proclaim the truth there is nothing more he can do but flee. This battle has already been won!

Psalm 20:6
Now I know that the Lord rescues his anointed king.
He will answer him from his holy heaven and rescue
him by his great power.

77. Rest in My Peace

O h, that you could fathom my love for you! Just open your heart and allow my healing rains to wash you and cleanse you from anything that is getting in the way of your freedom. My love is extending unto you from the heavens above and from deep within your heart where I reside.

You are a wonderful treasure to behold. Your heart is so precious to me.

Let me capture all of your anxieties and concerns within my hands so that you may experience peace that is unexplainable. The peace I give to you, I give to you in abundance. Rest in my peace and all will be well this day.

Romans 15:33
And now may God, who gives us his peace, be with
you all. Amen.

78. Call upon My Name

C ome and take part in my goodness that I offer all of my children who call upon my name. As you go about your day, remember to think about me. Simply say hello and let me know what is on your mind. I wait patiently for you because I love you.

I know the days can get very busy and it is easy to get distracted and forget about my presence. Some days are easier to walk with me than others. Some days you are so busy that you forget I am there to help lighten your load.

Simply call upon my name and I am there for you. Some days there are great challenges and struggles where all you can do is cry out to me for help. That is what I am here for, to help you and to guide you.

Whatever your day may hold, make a conscious effort to talk to me. A simple "Jesus!" is all it takes and I am there. I stand waiting for you to call on me. Let us walk through this day together and it will be well with your soul.

Acts 2:21
***But everyone who calls on the name of the Lord will
be saved.***

79. Come and Follow Me

*T*oday is a brand new day to call on me and invite me to walk and talk with you. You can talk with me about anything and everything. Nothing is insignificant to me.

As you talk to me and share your heart, my Spirit will speak to your spirit. I will shine a light into areas of darkness. I will bring you new insight and give you a different way of looking at the same situation. My Spirit within you will be your guide and I will bring you to higher grounds where you will have a broader view and greater perspective of the truth in your circumstances.

Come and follow me. I will make a way for you where there seems to be no way. With me, all things are possible. I am with you as your Helper. Lean on me when you are feeling weak and I will be your strength.

Matthew 16:24
Then Jesus said to his disciples, "If any of you wants
to be my follower, you must turn from your selfish
ways, take up your cross, and follow me."

80. I Hear You

Your hope in me is like a song that fills a heart with gladness. Your thankfulness for all I do in your life brings joy to my heart. I desire the very best for you in all things, in everything that you do. I will reveal myself to you as you press into me.

Do you know that I am your biggest advocate? I am the one who stands by your side at all times. When you are walking through a storm in life, just whisper my name. I hear you and am responding to your call. My Spirit will lead you in the way you should go as you keep your eyes focused on me.

Take a moment to remember all the times that I have been with you and helped you through. This will strengthen your faith and be an encouragement to you. Stand up and be proud. The heavens are cheering you on.

You have come so far along on your journey with me. You have been growing and learning in leaps and bounds along the way. Keep pressing forward. I admire you and am proud to call you Friend.

Psalm 4:3
You can be sure of this: The Lord set apart the godly
for himself. The Lord will answer when I call to him.

81. I Have Called You to Be a Light

Beloved One, allow my rivers of living waters to cleanse you and remove anything that gets in the way of our communion with each other. There is an anointing upon your life. I have called you to be a light unto my children—to lead the lost and broken out of captivity.

Allow my love to flow freely through you to others. I am increasing your compassion for my children and giving you a greater understanding of what it means to set the captives free.

Surrender your heart to me and I will cut the cords that have kept you bound and limited you from fully stepping into the ministry I have called you to. As you are set free, so shall my light within you set others free.

Isaiah 42:6
I, the Lord, have called you to demonstrate my
righteousness. I will take you by the hand and guard
you, and I will give you to my people, Israel, as a
symbol of my covenant with them. And you will be a
light to guide the nations.

82. My Word Is Food for Your Soul

Oh Sweet and Tender Child, how I long for you to sit at my feet and nourish your soul with my Word of life which is everlasting and true. As you commit your time to me you are sowing seeds of faith and will reap a harvest of righteousness. Be at peace and rest in me.

My hand of grace is upon you. Your feet are planted firmly on my Rock as you apply my Word to your daily life and walk in its truth. My Word is food for your soul. Step forth into this new day and walk with me. I am with you.

Hebrews 4:12
For the word of God is alive and powerful. It is sharper than the sharpest two-edged sword, cutting between soul and spirit, between joint and marrow. It exposes our innermost thoughts and desires.

83. Let Me Wipe the Tears

I can see the sadness in your eyes and feel the sorrow in your heart. Do you know how much I love you, Precious Child? Let me wipe the tears that are streaming down your cheeks. Allow me to embrace you with my loving presence which is all about you now.

I am here to bring you comfort. I am here to turn your thoughts that bring you sadness into thoughts that bring you joy.

Allow me to take this pain you are feeling deep inside and gently wash it away with my love. I will fill the emptiness you are experiencing within with the fullness of my love.

Lift up your head so that I may see your face, so that I may look into your eyes and tell you that I love you and that all will be well. Your sorrows will turn to joy as you see my hand of grace upon you.

My mercies are new every morning and each day brings new light. Rest in me as you release it all into my hands. I am right by your side and I will never let you go.

> **Lamentations 3:21-23**
> *Yet I still dare to hope when I remember this: The faithful love of the Lord never ends! His mercies never cease. Great is his faithfulness; his mercies begin afresh each morning.*

84. I Am the Rock

*W*alking in my light will bring you peace that strengthens your spirit. During the storms of life, come and walk with me. I will cover you with a spiritual umbrella that keeps you protected from the schemes of the enemy who would like nothing more than to knock you off the Rock and keep you from getting up.

What frustrates the enemy the most is that my children who are planted firmly on the Rock cannot be moved. No matter what the enemy brings your way, you will not be defeated. You may stumble, you may even fall at times, but my redemption goes before you and my strength in you gives you the power to overcome and rise back up again.

So take my hand and rise up with me. Walk with me to the mountaintop and I will open your eyes to see things like you have never seen them before—through my eyes. The rains will dry up. The dark clouds will drift away. My sun will shine upon your life and you will experience the calm that always comes after the storm. When you look beneath your feet, there you will see the Rock. You will see that I have been there with you all along.

2 Samuel 22:32-33
For who is God except the Lord? Who but our God is
a solid rock? God is my strong fortress, and he makes
my way perfect.

85. I Have Great Compassion for You

*W*hen you find yourself lost and abandoned by others, do not fear. Do not be sad, for my mercies are new every morning and I have great compassion for you. I see the hurt in your eyes and can feel the hurt in your heart. You can be confident that I will always come to your rescue, no matter what you are going through.

This may be a difficult day for you. Call out to me. I have much to share with you that will help you to be successful on your journey. Even when the path before you is filled with thorns and you do not know how to proceed, I will make the way for you.

You do not have to figure everything out this moment. My wisdom will pour over you as you are ready to receive the truth of my Word.

Do not be sad, my Child. I love you so.

Psalm 86:15
But you, O Lord, are a God of compassion and mercy,
slow to get angry and filled with unfailing love and
faithfulness.

86. Take Delight in Me

Take delight in me and I will give you the desires of your heart. As you direct your thoughts toward me, I will pour out upon you riches from heaven. As you are led by my Spirit within you, I will give you all you need exactly how you need it. What I do as your Shepherd is lead you in the way you should go.

You may feel at times as though I have not answered your prayers or that I am delayed in doing so. Be assured this day that I have heard all the cries of your heart. I have known every longing of your heart before you were even born. Imagine that. So when you come to me with requests, longings, and desires it is of no surprise to me.

When it seems as though I am delayed in answering, it is not because I have not heard you. My desire is that you have the very best. My answers often seem delayed, but as you seek after me and come to know me better you will realize that I am teaching you along the way how to trust in me.

Remember, as I speak of in my Word, that hope does not disappoint. As you put your trust in me, hope is alive and breathing new life within you. As you mature in your faith and continue to develop and grow your relationship with me, you will find that delighting in me also means trusting in me.

As you trust in me, you are laying yourself down and submitting to my perfect will. I am perfecting the desires of your heart to be in perfect alignment with my will. When your desire is in accord with my will and you have been made wholly ready to receive, it is then that you will begin to see your desires manifest in your life before your very eyes.

I am faithful to my Word and all of my promises are true and everlasting. Delight yourself in me and I will give you the desires of your heart.

Psalm 37:4
Take delight in the Lord, and he will give you your
heart's desires.

87. I Will Be with You Always

*L*ook deep within your heart and there will you find me. I sit, waiting to talk with you from the throne room I established in your heart when you asked me to become the Lord of your life.

You may remember the very moment you first took a leap of faith and called upon my name—your Jesus. Perhaps you have always held me in your heart but have come to know me in different ways through time and seasons, joys and sorrows.

It is not how you came to know me and when I became real to you that matters the most. What truly matters is that you do know me and believe in me. I suffered on the cross to redeem you so that you could live life eternally. I will be with you always.

John 17:3
And this is the way to have eternal life—to know you,
the only true God, and Jesus Christ, the one you sent
to earth.

88. My Glory Is Upon You!

S urrounding you are my guardian angels that I have appointed to watch over you. As you rest tonight I will go before you and orchestrate the rising of the sun to greet you in the morning hours.

There is a beautifully choreographed symphony of love flowing down upon you from the heavens. Cascades of pure and living waters are cleansing your heart and mind as your thoughts float into dreams.

The fragrance of my presence envelops your calm and tender spirit. Your humility shines like a radiant moonbeam lighting up the starry night skies.

The song I am singing over you will fill your heart with gladness and bring strength to your soul. A new and glorious day is arising.

Make way for the King of Kings! The trumpets sound and the angels sing. Behold! I am entering your heart this day for you to rise up as my ambassador to share my goodness with all those I place along your path.

Be of good cheer for you will radiate my light and all will see the magnificence of my love as you greet my children with a smile. My glory is upon you!

Psalm 3:3
But you, O Lord, are a shield around me; you are my
glory, the one who holds my head high.

89. I Am Raising Up a Standard against the Enemy

I am with you this day to edify you and lift you up. Come along and soar to new heights with me. I am raising up a standard against the enemy. Stand firm and push back against the darkness and break through with my light.

This battle you are in, whether it be small or seemingly insurmountable, you are not in it alone. You are never alone. You have the Creator of the universe standing by your side cheering you on to victory.

Never underestimate the power of my love. All you need to do is trust in me. Trust that my Word is true and everlasting. What I promised to my children in days of old are promises I made for you too, knowing the very time, very moment, very minute you would exist.

You are here for a purpose. I loved you into existence. It is true that you were created by my hand out of love. And you, just the way you are, imperfections and all, are my priceless masterpiece.

There is hidden treasure in you that is yet to be discovered. Just wait until you find what I have stored up for you in the treasuries of your heart. You will be utterly amazed.

You are amazing to me. Just as a parent smiles in adoration of their child, so do I beam with adoration over you.

Deuteronomy 20:4
For the Lord your God is going with you! He will fight
for you against your enemies, and he will give you
victory!

90. I Have You in the Palm of My Hand

You are my lovely, radiant flower, full of brilliant colors. My love surrounds your heart and very being. Even though you have internal struggles where your mind can rage in war with itself—I am the calming voice that brings you into the light and out of the darkness.

Your wisdom is growing as you seek to overcome areas in your life that have kept you locked into those cold, dark places. It only takes a tiny flame to bring light to a room. That is the flame you need to follow after, the light of my Holy Spirit—the fire of my righteousness and power. If all you can see is a tiny flicker of light, that is all the hope you need to hold on to for the day, for my light will see you through and you will make it out of the dark place.

Your struggles here are nothing in comparison to the glory that you will behold when I return. All of your efforts in putting your trust in me are not in vain. They define you. Your unwavering faithfulness brings adoration to my heart for you.

I look upon you with great admiration and compassion. Not one tear shed goes unnoticed by me. And those times when you are so in pain that you don't even have the energy to shed a tear—I know what you are feeling and going through. I have you in the palm of my hand.

You are more than a survivor; you are a conqueror! Great is the hand of the Almighty upon your life. Greatness shall go before you and follow you wherever you go.

Glorious Child, I love you so. Take my hand and walk with me. I have something special to show you this day.

Isaiah 49:16
See, I have written your name on the palms of my hands. Always in my mind is a picture of Jerusalem's walls in ruins.

91. I Have Overcome

*M*y Beloved Child, seek not after the things of this world. Seek after the gifts of the Spirit and treasures of the heart that are everlasting and true. Mighty is your Maker and wonderfully have you been made.

Oh, the many trials you have been through! You have been forged in the fire for a purpose far greater than you can imagine.

You have sought after me and my reward; one of my rewards is eternal and life-giving wisdom. Take this gift and share it with those who are walking the same walk. Share this gift to the lost and brokenhearted that have gone through many fiery trials. This is your testimony and the hope you give to others.

I have overcome so that you may overcome. You have overcome so that others may overcome. Rest assured that it has been worth the fight.

Be thankful for your trials for they shall bring you great strength in the days to come.

John 16:33
I have told you all this so that you may have peace
in me. Here on earth you will have many trials and
sorrows. But take heart, because I have overcome the
world.

92. I Will Rescue You

My goodness is flowing upon your life from the treasuries I have stored up for you in heaven. Each time that you call upon my name, trust in me. I will answer. I am coming. I am with you.

Many of your years have been laden with sorrows and your cries have pierced my heart. I look upon you with great compassion and want you to believe that everything will work out.

Not everything in this life of yours will go perfectly. This is a fallen world, but I have come to restore and redeem my beloved children. You are my Beloved Child and I will rescue you.

Psalm 18:19
He led me to a place of safety; he rescued me because
he delights in me.

93. *Rest upon My Shoulders*

*T*here are times when you may feel weary, worn out, or burdened. There are times when you make poor choices. There are times when you feel like giving up or throwing in the towel. These are the times you especially need to press into me.

Do not continue condemning yourself for things you have done wrong. You are forgiven, my Child. Now, come, let us lay out a new path together. Consider us a team. I am here to coach you and to lead you into greater things.

You may get tired along the way, but I ask that you do not give up. Remember, it is darkest before the dawn. You never know what glory the next day may behold.

Rest upon my shoulders and allow me to recharge your battery, to re-energize your spirit so you can continue upward on your journey. I will lighten your load and bring peace to you this day as you turn it all over to me.

Matthew 11:28
Then Jesus said, "Come to me, all of you who are weary and carry heavy burdens, and I will give you rest."

94. I Gave My Son

The way into my heart is through loving and through prayer. When you pray, it is an act of faith. Your prayer is also an act of love. Come! Sit by my side and talk with me. Express your heart and deepest thoughts. I am listening.

As you let down your walls and expose your vulnerabilities to me, I can begin to penetrate those dark and troublesome areas with my light. My light will bring healing. The deeper your prayer life is with me, the deeper our relationship grows.

Moment by moment, layer by layer I will uncover anything that keeps you from being closer to me. I will reveal to you truths about yourself. Once the truth is unveiled, you will be able to see yourself from a new vantage point. You will begin to see yourself the way I see you.

I want you to know how deep and wide is my love for you and that nothing can separate you from my love. My love for you flows like a river that will never dry up.

Imagine trying to wrap your arms around the ocean. It would seem impossible to grasp something so great in your arms. But what you may not realize is that an entire ocean is but a tiny drop of water compared to the gift you now hold in your heart. I gave my Son so that he may live and reign in your heart forever.

So remember, when you enter into prayer you are talking to the King of all Kings and you have my undivided attention. Nothing is insignificant to me. If it matters to you, it matters to me for I take each and every one of your concerns to heart.

John 3:16
***For this is how God loved the world: He gave his one
and only Son, so that everyone who believes in him
will not perish but have eternal life.***

95. I Am Calling You Higher and Higher

My Beloved Child, as you seek my face I will in turn open the heavens unto you, giving you access to the glorious mysteries of my kingdom. As your heart and mind are enlightened, your understanding of my Word will increase exponentially. This will open doors in your life that you never realized were even there.

My light will shine upon the path before you and you will see things like you have never seen them before. You will be able to take your newfound wisdom and apply it to your daily life. This will enable you to overcome obstacles that have impeded your growth and forward momentum.

You will wake up singing new and glorious praises unto your Father who has brought you new light to brighten your day. You will receive a greater awareness of who you are in my eyes and all that I have called you to be.

I am calling you higher and higher. Go forth and bring my light into the world this day.

2 Corinthians 3:18
So all of us who have had that veil removed can see
and reflect the glory of the Lord. And the Lord—who
is the Spirit—makes us more and more like him as we
are changed into his glorious image.

96. I Eagerly Anticipate the Moments We Share Together

Never has there been a time or place where I have not existed, for I am in all things, with all things, and have given all things. In days to come, the light of my love will overpower the lost and the broken in ways that have never been known to man. I am a God who loves you beyond compare. I would have it that all of my children draw near me so that I can empower them to live righteously and to walk with blessing and goodness surrounding them.

I want for you to know that I am a merciful God, and even if you feel as though you are not where you would like to be in relationship with me, know that it is never too late.

Today is the day to begin, and remember that every day as you awake is a new day. I eagerly anticipate the moments we share together. I love the daily conversations we have with each other. The more time you spend developing a relationship with me, the closer we will become. As with everything, the more you put into it, the more you get out of it.

Love me with all of your heart, mind, strength, and soul and in doing so I will teach you how to love others the way they deserve to be loved. I love all my children and there is not one soul that is not precious in my eyes.

My heart is saddened when my children deny my name and walk through their lives as if they do not need me. I daily give my children the opportunity to rely on me, to trust in me, to walk with me.

As you walk with me—I walk with you. Even when you do not feel my presence, know that I am always by your side. Never once have I forsaken those who belong to me.

In times to come, as you call upon my name, you will see a change in the atmosphere around you—a change in the attitudes of my children as I give them new understanding of my undying love for them.

Today as you call upon my name, know that you are loved. I give my children what they need. Give your very best to me and I will always give my very best to you.

Psalm 42:1
As the deer longs for streams of water, so I long for you, O God.

97. *I Am True to My Word Always*

My heart goes out to you this day. Whenever you feel afraid, run to me and I will shelter you in my arms. Do not fear for I am with you always. I watch over you with loving kindness.

Sometimes you are overcome with thoughts that seem to set your mind in a tail spin. During these times focus not on the issues that pervade your thoughts. Instead, release those thoughts into my hands. Focus not on your concerns. Focus on me.

Ponder on the greatness and majesty of your God, your Almighty Father. I am true to my Word always.

You may feel at times that I have not followed through on my promises. I have. There is a time and season for all things. When it is the right time, my perfect time, you will see my light. I will reveal to you my purpose and perfect will.

Do not lose heart. Keep your eyes fixed on me and in time you will receive your reward. My blessings and peace are ever before you. Just continue to press in and keep your eyes and heart focused on me and my presence.

Rest in me today and it will be well with your soul.

Psalm 33:4
For the word of the Lord holds true, and we can trust everything he does.

98. I Will Shower You with My Loving Kindness

Today as you look to me, I will shower you with my loving kindness. Even when your heart is troubled, know that I am with you.

When you are searching for answers deep within your heart, know that you are going to find those answers as you direct your thoughts toward me. Trying to figure all the details out on your own will only cause anxiety.

I would have it that you turn toward me. I would have it that you experience peace. I am the Master Architect of your life and I am building something great and new within you this season.

Be refreshed this day and rest assured that I love you and am working on your behalf, in all circumstances. Turn your face toward me, my Beloved, so that I may give you a smile that melts your heart. I am smiling upon you this day.

Jeremiah 31:3
Long ago the Lord said to Israel: "I have loved you,
my people, with an everlasting love. With unfailing
love I have drawn you to myself."

99. I Will Never Leave You

Treasure of my Heart, I love you. My love for you is deep and wide. It extends to the heavens and beyond. My love for you has no end. I have loved you always. You are never outside of my love.

I know that at times it is difficult for you to receive my love. This happens when you are down on yourself and discouraged. I want you to open your heart to me at these times and let my love surround you. This will bring healing and restoration.

My love for you lifts you up. It brings you to a place where you can be confident that I am with you.

I know that you feel alone sometimes, and there are many who feel alone all the time. You are never alone.

Why is it that you do not always feel my presence? Because it is in these times that I am refining you and calling you to deeper places. When you do not feel me, you come looking for me more fervently. And as you seek me, you shall find me. I will never leave you.

You may feel like you are in the dark, but I am the light within you that keeps you moving forward. I am your hope.

Be encouraged in my love for you. I give it to you in great measure. Oh, that you could fathom my love for you! One day, you will. That day is on its way. Be ready for it, for it will take many by surprise if they are not seeking after me.

Treasure of my Heart—I love you.

Deuteronomy 31:8
Do not be afraid or discouraged, for the Lord will personally go ahead of you. He will be with you; he will neither fail you nor abandon you.

100. *The Power of My Word*

*B*eloved One, I have come so that you may find rest. The days of your life at times can be exhausting. I know this. I am here to refresh your spirit and give you the energy you need to make it through your busy days.

In the midst of it all, remember to pause and look up to me. I will give you what you need to weather any storm that comes your way.

Some days you will walk with confidence and surety in me. Other days, because of the enemy's wicked ways, you may be bombarded with negative thoughts that bring you down. Be aware that these thoughts do not come from me.

When this occurs, draw upon my Word and speak the truth over yourself. My Word will break through any wall that the enemy tries to surround you with. Do you know the power of my Word? It is life giving and will empower you to walk in my ways despite your circumstances.

Be refreshed in me. I am your greatest advocate and I have your best interests at heart at all times. My arms are wide open. Let me embrace you with my love this day. All will be well.

Psalm 33:6
The Lord merely spoke, and the heavens were created.
He breathed the word, and all the stars were born.

101. I Am Coming Soon

Y ou are a prized pearl in my kingdom. You have walked down a path that very few have journeyed. You have been brave. Your journey to my heart has lifted you up to a new vantage point where you are now able to see far beyond what you ever thought you could see.

I give you glimpses of my glory as you invite me in to dwell with you. These glimpses are the sparks of hope that I keep alive within your heart.

Oh, your hope in victory is just the beginning. I have called you to be with me in a new way. When I move, there is nothing that can get in my way.

There is a tidal wave of my love coming in the near future that will hit the land with force. Anyone who is in the way of this move of the Spirit will be impacted deep within their hearts, both believers in me and non-believers. It will be a day of reckoning.

I will show you things in the realm of my Spirit that will lead you in the way you should go. Be not afraid, for I am doing a good thing in the land. There will be a fresh anointing on my chosen ones, and I will impart to them many new gifts that will help them to call my children home.

I want you to know that you are and always will be in the palm of my hand. You cannot be moved for I am your Rock. I am your firm foundation.

Cling to me and I will make a way for you in the desert. I will be your refreshing spring of life-giving waters. Read my Word. Sing my Word. Listen to my Word. Are you ready? I am coming soon.

Revelation 22:12
Look, I am coming soon, bringing my reward with me
to repay all people according to their deeds.

102. *You Will Be Victorious in Me*

O h, Sweet and Beloved Friend of mine, how I long to have you sit at my feet and listen to me. I have so much to share with you about yourself. What I have to share will bring you all the hope in the world that you need to make it through the day.

When you feel like you have been abandoned, know that I am with you. I am nearer to you than you can even imagine. As you look up to me, I am looking upon you with great admiration. I want you to know that, despite the odds, you will be victorious in me and through me.

Remember that I will always make a way for you where there seems to be no way. I am setting the course by which you can run across the finish line and win the prize I have been waiting to give all of my children who keep their heart and minds focused on me. I am the one who brings life and freedom.

You are well on your way to victory. Stay the course, my Friend. I am with you always.

Psalm 91:14-16
The Lord says, "I will rescue those who love me. I will
protect those who trust in my name. When they call on
me, I will answer; I will be with them in trouble.
I will rescue and honor them. I will reward them with
a long life and give them my salvation."

103. I Am About to Do a New Thing in Your Life

Oh, Beloved! Let your heart pour forth in songs of joy this day for I am about to do a new thing in your life! I am right by your side longing to share with you the mysteries of my kingdom, the wonders of my love for you, and the beautiful treasure you are to me.

Press into me and I will fulfill the desires of your heart. I will give you so much more than you ever hoped or dreamed of because I love you so much. Your pure devotion to me captures my heart. You radiate with light when you spend time in my presence, for I reside deep within your heart and I am light.

Do not worry today for I will carry you through. You are not alone in this. Whatever unfolds throughout your day, know that I am pouring out my love upon your heart. Be at peace and rest assured that I will fight for you and you will be victorious!

Stand strong, be courageous, be bold, be brave! You can do this. I believe in you!

Joshua 1:9
This is my command—be strong and courageous! Do not be afraid or discouraged. For the Lord your God is with you wherever you go.

104. You Are Perfect in My Eyes

*T*ake heart, my Beloved, for I am about to do something unexpected in your life that will bring you joy beyond compare. You have sat at my feet night after night calling upon my name and I have heard every cry of your heart. Weep no more, my Beloved. It is a new day.

I have laid out a path for your life that will have you singing songs of praise all day long. Do you see it? Can you feel it?

Oh, that you would know how deeply I love you. You are not inadequate—you are perfect in my eyes. The blood of my Son covers all inadequacy. You are a conqueror through my Son who made all things possible for you. Reach out and take my hand.

Let me lead you to new horizons, to places you've never even dreamed of going. I have so much to show you. You will be my mouthpiece and your words through my Spirit will break the chains of those who are bound up and broken. I will set people free through my love that is burning brightly within you.

I have called you this day. Do you hear my call? Do you trust me? Oh Sweet Child, all you have to do is be who you are for you are perfect in my eyes. I will lead the way. Come and follow me!

Luke 4:18-19
The Spirit of the Lord is upon me, for he has anointed me to bring Good News to the poor. He has sent me to proclaim that captives will be released, that the blind will see, that the oppressed will be set free, and that the time of the Lord's favor has come.

105. You Are My Perfect Masterpiece

*B*eloved One, you are my perfect masterpiece! You have all it takes to be victorious in this life for I am with you. You will face challenges in life but you will not be overcome. I will fight on your behalf and give you the strength you need to face any trial that comes your way.

Come! Draw near to me and I will give you new insight and wisdom that will lead you down the right path. Be bold, be courageous! Step out of the boat and walk on the water with me. You have nothing to fear. Press forward in faith and I will give you the desires of your heart!

Deuteronomy 31:6
So be strong and courageous! Do not be afraid and do not panic before them. For the Lord your God will personally go ahead of you. He will neither fail you nor abandon you.

106. I Am Perfect Love

My love for you transcends time. I have always loved you and will love you forever. Pour out your heart to me this day, my Beloved. Reach out and take my hand and I will lift you up to places your eyes have not yet seen. My Spirit is alive and flourishing deep within your heart. I am at home within your heart because you have invited me in.

When you invite me in a veil is lifted and the union between our hearts is nourished. We share a deep bond with each other because you have dedicated your life to me. You have heard me call you in the night hours and you have responded with joy.

I anticipate each moment you call upon my name. My name spoken through your lips is music to my ears—it is a sweet love song that fills my heart with undeniable passion for you.

My love for you is like a river flowing through the valleys, strong and swift. My love for you is like the wings of an eagle soaring through the sky. My love for you is like the glow of brilliant colors in a sunset on a warm night. My love never escapes you. It is real. It is alive. My love is at the center of your heart and within the depths of your soul.

Come fly away with me into your dreams and let me reveal to you my destiny for your life, the purpose for which I created you. You will walk in amazement when you see the plans I have for you. You will sing praises and shout for joy as I pour out my love upon you.

Seek me and you will find me. I am all that you need. I am perfect love.

2 Corinthians 13:14
May the grace of the Lord Jesus Christ, the love of God,
and the fellowship of the Holy Spirit be with you all.

107. I Am Here to Fill Your Heart with Peace

*B*eloved One, I am calling you to come sit at my feet and listen to me share words of wisdom with you. I will guide your daily steps and give you insight into my Word. Whenever the enemy tries to rob your peace, ignore him and look to me. I will re-focus your thoughts on heavenly things. He cannot exist in my presence so when you are in communion with me, he has to flee.

I desire to spend time with you one on one—just you and me. If you can set aside some time each day to do that I will bless you in ways you have never imagined. I have so many things on my heart that I long to share with you. Most importantly I want you to know how greatly you are loved by me and how proud I am of you.

I know you doubt yourself at times, but do not doubt my love for you—it never changes. I reside within your heart—that is where you will find me when you come to spend time with me.

I am here to fill your heart with peace, joy, and love. I am sending people into your life who will share in your enthusiasm for heavenly things, people who share in your love for me and my Father. When you spend time with those people whose hearts are focused on me, I will ignite a flame of passion within you to serve my Father daily. You will revel together in all that I am doing in your lives and about how much you have to look forward to.

I am sending you new blessings today. Get ready to receive blessings in abundance like never before. I am with you. I am for you. And I adore you.

Jude 1:2
May God give you more and more mercy, peace, and love.

108. Hold On to the Hope I Have Given You

S weet Child, how I long to have you sit in my presence and soak in my majesty. You are wonderful in the sight of your Maker. You have made tremendous strides in your journey to my heart. You are an overcomer. With me you are victorious. Your life shall bring glory to my name.

I care for all your needs, big and small. I am your Protector. I am your Great Provider. No one shall thwart the plans I have for your life for I have called you by name. You are mine. You are chosen. You belong to the Almighty One.

Songs of deliverance and freedom are flowing down from the heavens above to rest upon your heart this day. Receive this music as a sweet comfort to your heart. Joy in great measure I am giving to you, my Child.

Righteousness and truth are presiding over your heart and mind. Wisdom into the things that are incomprehensible will give you new insight and revelation. Listen to that still, small voice within your heart that tells you which way to turn at every crossroad in your life.

Pour out your heart to those who come running to you longing to know me. I will show you how much love I hold in my heart for all my dear ones. I want to bless you for your faithfulness and trust in me. Receive all that I send you in the way of love and comfort from those I place in your midst.

You do not always have to be strong. Let me be strong for you. Your strength in me will in turn give you the rest you desire. The peace that you long for will envelop your heart and soul every day as you rest in me.

Bring all your concerns to me and I will break every area of bondage and every stronghold that tries to get in the way of the blessed life that I hold in my hand just for you. I am your Mighty Savior, and you are my precious child of resiliency. Hold on to the hope I have given you; it shall never disappoint you.

Psalm 71:14
But I will keep on hoping for your help; I will praise
you more and more.

109. Call on Me When You Feel Weak

*B*ehold! A new day is dawning! Let your past failures go. Look forward to what I have to bring into your future that will be filled with my light and love. My compassion is ever before you. I know when you are discouraged and I am here to lift you up.

I am thrilled when you experience joy—it brings a smile to my face. I am so proud of you and happy to call you my Friend and Child; you are the beloved of my heart.

Come! Be my companion in this journey of life. Walk with me. Talk with me. Let me pour my Spirit upon you as you soak in my Word, which will bring you comfort and shine a light in the darkness.

Today and every day I stand by your side. I will bring you from glory to glory. Just trust in me. Call on me when you are feeling weak and I will give you strength.

I leave you with one parting thought this hour. Every time you go through a storm and keep your faith in me, you are growing stronger in my love. I love you and am praying to the Father on your behalf every moment of your life. You are blessed!

John 17:24
Father, I want these whom you have given me to be with me where I am. Then they can see all the glory you gave me because you loved me even before the world began!

110. I Am Placing a New Love Song in Your Heart

*B*eloved Child, come running to me with eyes wide open like a little child and experience the glory of my presence. Let all the worries of the day fall off of your shoulders and rest in me. I will sing sweet songs of love over you. I will tell you just how much I love you. I will pour out my love and grace upon your life.

If you ever wonder where I am, look no further—you will find me deep within your heart. I wait for you to come and talk to me.

You have things that are weighing upon your heart—share them with me. Open up to me and let it all out. As you share, you will feel the weight of those burdens start to lighten. I will bring a refreshing peace to your heart.

I want you to know that you are my prize possession and I am building a mansion just for you in heaven. You will be amazed when you behold it with your eyes. I know this life can be hard, but rest assured that you have an eternal inheritance coming that will blow your mind—it is glorious!

I am placing a new love song in your heart. Listen to that still, small voice rising up from within. I will be with you as you go about your day today. I will be walking right by your side.

Psalm 42:8
But each day the Lord pours his unfailing love upon me, and through each night I sing his songs, praying to God who gives me life.

111. I Will Never Let You Go

*D*earest Beloved, here I stand at the door of your heart and knock. Open wide your heart and receive my love.

I know at times the battles of life are overwhelming. Fear not, for I am right by your side and will be your guide through the stormy nights.

As a new day has dawned, anticipate my goodness to overflow in your life. When you are unsure about what the future holds, rest in this thought—I am with you. No matter what happens, I will never let you go.

At times you may feel as though you have lost your footing, but in those times call upon my name and I will lift you up to higher grounds. I have so much goodness to pour out upon your life. When you have doubts or fears, come running to me and I will give you rest and will reassure you that all will be well.

Be encouraged this day for my love for you is beyond compare. I will keep you on the right path as you call upon my name. My Beloved, open wide your heart and receive my love. All that I have is yours.

Psalm 23:6
Surely your goodness and unfailing love will pursue me
all the days of my life, and I will live in the house of the
Lord forever.

112. Be at Peace This Hour

*D*earest Beloved Child, I know you are longing for closeness to me. I know you have been seeking after me and looking for the path I have laid out for you. It is right before you, just wait on me. I am with you and am leading you down the right path. Just the fact that you are seeking after me is enough—that is what I ask of you right now.

Be strong and courageous! Keep pressing forward in your journey to my heart and I will pour blessings over you like you've never experienced before. You are doing well. You may not see the end from the beginning right now, but I do, and I am taking you by the hand now and will show you the way.

Be at peace this hour. I am right by your side.

Psalm 21:6
You have endowed him with eternal blessings and
given him the joy of your presence.

113. Take My Hand and Let Me Lead You by Still Waters

Dearest Beloved, you are my precious one. I look upon you with great admiration. As you call upon my name, I am there. I never leave your side. When you doubt, come to me and I will reassure you that all will be well. You are in my care and I have charged my angels to watch over you and protect you.

Be not weary this day. Though the road may be rough and obstacles are in your way, you will make it to your destination, to a place where you and I will never be apart. There is no division in my kingdom of heaven. There is only unity and oneness with your Creator. I am standing strong on your behalf and my prayers are always with you.

Take my hand today and let me lead you beside still waters. Rest in my love and I will show you just how much I love you. A new day is dawning, a day of new beginnings and joy. You will make it through this. Just hold my hand and keep me near to your heart. I will never let you down.

Things may not always go as you had planned, but just remember—I have a better plan for your life. All will be well, this I promise you.

Psalm 91:11-12
For he will order his angels to protect you wherever you go. They will hold you up with their hands so you won't even hurt your foot on a stone.

114. Stand Strong, You Will Get through This

*B*eloved Child, do you ever wonder why you are going through sufferings and hardship? That is the world you live in and the very reason that I suffered for you—to ultimately set you free. There will always be hardships and struggles in this world but I want you to know that I am with you. I never leave your side.

Sometimes you feel so alone in it all. You are never alone. That is where faith comes in. That is where hope lives. One day, my Child, your sufferings will no longer exist and you will live an eternal life free of pain and filled with joy beyond compare.

Stand strong, you will get through this and will walk into a brighter day once again.

Job 11:18
Having hope will give you courage. You will be
protected and will rest in safety.

115. You Are the Treasure of My Heart

*T*reasure of my heart, I look upon you this day with great admiration. You are highly esteemed in my eyes. Every time you think of me, I am filled with great joy. It is my greatest pleasure to spend time conversing with you—listening to your prayers, sharing with you my love.

Today, no matter what it holds, remember this—I am walking right by your side. If you turn to the right, I will be there. If you turn to the left, I will be there. Lean on me for strength and I will satisfy your spirit with renewed peace and hope.

Each day is a new journey. Take it one step at a time. Your greatest destination is my heart; make sure you come and visit every day!

Matthew 6:21
Wherever your treasure is, there the desires of your heart will also be.

116. Anticipate My Blessings on Your Life

*B*eloved Friend—you are the joy of my heart. All that I am rejoices within me each and every time you call upon my name. Your praises are glorious, beautiful music to my ears. I am overflowing with thankfulness that you heard my call and have invited me to be a part of your life. I have so much to give to you this day—everything I have is yours.

Oh, the glory you will experience when I call you home to your eternal life with me in the presence of my Father. The mansion I am building on your behalf is personally, passionately, and lovingly created just for you. I have a perfect mansion in heaven designed just for you. I look forward to the day when I can take your hand and walk you through its entrance. I guarantee you will be overwhelmed and utterly amazed, for your mansion was built out of perfect love.

I am sending you a special gift of my love this day—anticipate my blessings upon your life for they are coming. Hold on to hope, rejoice in love, and one day we will dine together in an eternal paradise built on the foundation of my Father's love for all His children.

I love you beyond compare and I want for you to know this moment that you are perfect in my eyes. My love I send you now. My peace I give unto you. You are blessed and I will forever hold you in my loving arms.

John 14:2
There is more than enough room in my Father's home. If this were not so, would I have told you that I am going to prepare a place for you?

117. Look to Me and I Will Help You

*I*n the midst of your trials, I am here. In the midst of your pain, I am here to ease your sufferings. In the midst of your worries, I am here to relieve the anxiousness you may be experiencing inside. Look to me and I will help you. I will show you a way out of the dark place.

Be not weary, my Child—just rest your head upon my shoulder and let me soothe you with my love. It will not always be this difficult. This is a temporary valley you have found yourself in. Take my hand and let me walk you up to the mountain top where you will see my glory in a different light.

I am showering my love down upon you this hour and bringing you a new, refreshing rain to renew your spirit and bring a smile to your face. Look up to me and I will give you all that you need to make it through this day and the days to come.

I love you beyond compare. You are my treasure.

Psalm 121:1-2
I look up to the mountains—does my help come from there? My help comes from the Lord, who made heaven and earth!

118. Be Patient and Continue to Trust in Me

I am listening to you, my Child. I know the concerns that are weighing upon your heart today. I am here to help you. I am here to guide you—to lead you down the right path. Rest assured that I have a perfect plan for your situation. You may not see it right now, but it is coming soon.

Be patient and continue to trust in me and I will make a way for you. In your weakest moments, when you are filled with doubt and hopelessness, I am the voice within you that says, "Keep pressing forward! You can get through this. I am right by your side."

You may know friends or family who are going through trying times but do not know how to help. You are helping every time you lift them up in prayer. I capture every one of your prayers in my heart and will move on their behalf as you ask of me.

In time, you will see the power of my love and see how I can move the mountains that stand in the way. I will show you a way around the mountain or over it. Just take my hand and walk with me. I will guide your every step.

2 Thessalonians 1:11-12
So we keep on praying for you, asking our God to enable you to live a life worthy of his call. May he give you the power to accomplish all the good things your faith prompts you to do. Then the name of our Lord Jesus will be honored because of the way you live, and you will be honored along with him. This is all made possible because of the grace of our God and Lord, Jesus Christ.

119. I Have Not Forgotten You

*D*o you feel like I am far away? I am nearer to you than you can imagine. Do you feel like I am not answering your prayers? I am answering your prayers, my Child. Please be patient for it must be in my timing for everything to come together the way it should be.

Do you feel like I have forgotten about you? I have not forgotten about you. You are always at the forefront of my mind.

It's a new day! I extend my heart to you this hour with great compassion and love. I hear the cries of your heart. I hear your prayers. I am always listening to you. I am working on your behalf behind the scenes to help you and your circumstances. Worry not this day for I am at the helm and am charting the course for you.

I am pleased with you. I hear you calling upon my name and this brings my heart great joy. The angels in the heavens rejoice with you today— they rejoice every time one of my lost children invites me to be a part of their lives.

You may have lost hope that your loved ones will be drawn into my kingdom and experience eternal salvation through me. Do not give up hope, my Child. Continue to pray for them. Remember, I leave the ninety-nine sheep to find the one who has been lost. It is a celebration in the heavens when the lost find their way home. I welcome all those who call upon my name.

I extend forgiveness to all who come to me asking for forgiveness. My Child, I forgive you for all your sins as you ask of me. Do not condemn yourself for your sins—that is what the enemy would have you do to keep you down. I have come to set you free, to purify your heart, to cleanse your spirit, and to wash you white as snow.

Rest in my arms today and I will give you peace.

Luke 12:6-7
What is the price of five sparrows—two copper coins?
Yet God does not forget a single one of them. And the
very hairs on your head are all numbered. So don't
be afraid; you are more valuable to God than a whole
flock of sparrows.

120. I Have the Answers You Need

Whenever you have doubt, come to me. Whenever you are anxious, come to me. Whenever you don't have the answers, come to me. I am here for you. I will wash away your doubt as you take your eyes off the problem as you focus on me. I will remove your anxiousness as you seek my face. I have the answers you need to guide you through your days; just seek after me and you will find me.

Be mindful to take some quiet time by yourself and sit in my presence. Talk to me and listen—I have much to share with you. Let down those walls and allow me into your heart. I will bring a new, refreshing wind to your sail that will move you forward in the right direction, steady and sure.

Come to me, my Child—take my hand and I will show you a brighter day and fill you with new hope. You have much to look forward to. My peace and grace I rest upon you this hour.

John 14:26
But when the Father sends the Advocate as my representative—that is, the Holy Spirit—he will teach you everything and will remind you of everything I have told you.

121. You Are Chosen

My Word is full of life and is there for you to draw on to receive guidance for your days, hope for your tomorrows, and joy for your today. I encourage you to draw from my wellspring of life that lives within you through my Holy Spirit. You may not realize how close I am to you. My Father sent the Holy Spirit so that you and I could have everlasting communion with each other until the day I call my children home.

If you have come up against an obstacle today, rest assured I will lead you in the way you should go. I have so much joy stored up for you in the treasuries of heaven. I anticipate every time you call upon my name.

I love to converse with you, to teach you, to help you get through the difficult days. When you sing praises to my Father, all the angels rejoice and great joy abounds in my heart and my Father's heart.

Keep on believing and trusting in me. I will shine a light upon your path and fill your heart with gladness. I love you beyond compare. I am coming soon. Take up your cross daily and follow me.

This life is nothing in comparison to the eternal joy you will experience when my children are united to me in the holy presence of my Father in heaven. Keep on pressing forward. I have called you for greatness. You are chosen. You are my child. You are my treasure. My heart is full of compassion for you.

Reach out and take my hand. Come and follow me and I will bring you new joy. I am with you now. I am with you always. I always have been and I always will be.

Deuteronomy 7:6
For you are a holy people, who belong to the Lord your God. Of all the people on earth, the Lord your God has chosen you to be his own special treasure.

122. My Word Is Your Shelter in the Storm

When the storms of life rage about you, call upon my name and I will be there. I know and understand your pain and the circumstances you are in. It is hard for my people to understand why there is much turmoil and chaos going on in the world around them.

I want your eyes to be opened today so that you have a greater opportunity to fight the battle that you may find yourself in—if not today, then in times to come for there will always be battles for you to fight whether it be little ones or big ones.

The first thing for you to recognize is that you are not only battling against flesh and blood—you are battling against the enemy of this world and his cohorts. This is something that so many of my children do not understand.

So many times my children call out to me in the midst of their trials and do not recognize the power that they have through me to slay the dragon. Your power comes through me and my Word. If you do not know my Word, then get to know my Word for this will give you so much strength to battle through the storms. My very Word is your shelter in the storm. It gives you the ability to calm the waters that are pulling you under.

If my children only recognized the power of my Word, victory would come so much sooner. When you think you are only battling against the people in your lives who are causing you pain, you are mistaken. There is always a spiritual battle that is going on, which is where the greatest confusion occurs.

It is the spiritual battles that bring people into depression. They come disguised in the form of negative, disparaging thoughts that cause you to dislike yourself and the people around you. The enemy speaks words of death around you in the spiritual realm, which wreaks havoc on your mind and brings you into a tailspin that pulls you under.

I only speak words of life. My Child, pull out your Bible—my Word of truth—and immerse yourself in it. Speak aloud my truths and you shall see walls fall down around you which will open up your perspective and give you the ability to find your way out of bondage.

When you feel trapped, open up my Word and you will find the truth that will set you free. My Word contains all that you need to know to cause the enemy to flee. If you are in a storm today, first call upon my name, then submit to me and send the enemy to flight through the power of my Word. This, my Dear One, will change your life and the circumstances around you.

I am the way, the truth, and the life and I have come to set you free!

Ephesians 6:12
For we are not fighting against flesh-and-blood
enemies, but against evil rulers and authorities of
the unseen world, against mighty powers in this dark
world, and against evil spirits in the heavenly places.

123. Cling to Me and I Will Protect You from the Storms of Life

I am holding on to you. Cling to me and I will protect you from the storms of life. Whenever you feel afraid, call upon my name and I will come running to you. It is possible through me to experience peace that surpasses all understanding while you are going through the storm.

I am the light within you that casts away the darkness. I am the light within you that shines brightly before others. As you remain in my presence during the storms, others will see your strength.

You may not recognize the strength within you as you feel weakened by the trials you are facing but know this—others will see your strength and be encouraged. You will bring hope to others who are going through trials. You are not alone in your sufferings. There are many who are suffering all around you.

The enemy works diligently to knock you off course. He wants to rob your peace and joy. He wants you to fall into sin and make you condemn yourself as his voice of condemnation weighs down your heart and mind. I am with you to set you free from any bondage that the enemy traps you with.

Be of good courage this day, my Child, for I am about to do a new thing in your life as you trust in me. It will not always be this difficult. This trial is temporary. No matter how long the trial has lasted, know that there will be an end to it and you will once again walk with joy in your heart.

I am proud of you that you haven't given up on me and that you haven't given up on yourself. You are my priceless masterpiece and I adore you. I will take care of you and guide your every step as you seek after me and seek after righteousness. I will make a way for you where there seems to be no way.

Rest in my love this day. You are loved.

Philippians 4:6-7
Don't worry about anything; instead, pray about
everything. Tell God what you need, and thank him
for all he has done. Then you will experience God's
peace, which exceeds anything we can understand.
His peace will guard your hearts and minds as you
live in Christ Jesus.

124. I Am Doing a Good Work within You During This Time

*A*s you follow my footsteps, I will help you to walk in righteousness—to walk in holiness before me. I am the one who will never leave you or forsake you. You may be experiencing negative thoughts that are bringing you down. It is not I who would speak negative thoughts to you—that is the enemy who is working against you to keep you from experiencing peace and joy.

The enemy wants to consume you with thoughts of failure and make you feel as though you are unlovable. He wants to consume you with lies about yourself and has a sneaky way of making it feel as if these thoughts are coming from yourself.

Do not fear for I am with you to help you rise above this negativity. One of the best ways you can begin to overcome these thoughts is to start singing praises to me and my Father. This can be a challenging thing to start when you are feeling down on yourself but it will help you to rise above the negativity almost the moment you start worshiping.

Thank me for your current sufferings—this will break the bondage of the enemy for the enemy cannot exist where you are inhabited with my praises. Once you have entered into this moment of worship—begin talking to me and tell me how you are feeling. I am listening and will begin to minister to your heart in a soothing way that will bring you comfort.

In this moment, allow me to speak truth to your spirit—truth about who you really are in me, which is the opposite of what the enemy speaks to you. Rest in my love.

Taking this time to worship will help you to break loose of the enemy's bondage and transform your mind. I will replace the negative thoughts about yourself with positive thoughts.

Be patient with yourself. I am doing a good work within you during this time. Always remember that I am with you. I will never leave your side.

Psalm 5:12
For you bless the godly, O Lord; you surround them
with your shield of love.

125. Keep Your Faith and Hope Alive In Me

*T*oday is a brand new day! It is my gift to you. As you think on all that you need to do this day, remember that I will be with you as you call upon my name.

These last several days, months, or even years may have been laden with great challenges. It may seem as though you are not having victory and that your prayers have not been answered.

I want you to know that I have heard all the cries of your heart. I do answer your prayers but oftentimes my answers may not come in the form you were hoping for or expecting.

Remember, my ways are higher than your ways and ultimately my perfect purpose for your life will prevail as you follow after me—it can take time so please be patient with yourself and patient with me. Do not worry.

As you continue to seek after me, I will show you what you need to do to be victorious in your battles. I am working within you during this time to transform your mind and teach you how to face your trials with new strength.

As you persevere through your trials, you are building strength of character. This is a good thing that will serve you well in the days to come. You may feel like you cannot handle the situation you are currently in but you can with my help.

You do not have to figure everything out. Some answers to prayers come quickly; some take some time for there are many variables to each person's circumstances. When I am working within you and others to restore and rebuild relationships, it can take time for forgiveness and healing needs to take place in order for you to have total freedom and peace.

As you endure these trials, know that there is always a beginning and end to everything. There was a beginning to your trial and there will be an end to your trial. Keep your faith and hope alive in me and you will win this battle for I am with you.

I am the light within you that gives you strength even in the midst of the storms that can rage about you. I know that you need me and I want you to know I am with you to take care of all your needs.

Be patient, my Child. In the end, all will be well and you will enter into a place of wholeness. Even in your sufferings you can experience peace and joy through me. Let me show you the way to think like me. This will help you to know which way to turn at each crossroad. I am alive and living within you.

Take my hand and we will forge through this valley and walk up to the mountaintop where your testimony will bring hope and life to many who are going through similar trials. Enter into this day with new hope. I am with you.

Jeremiah 7:23
This is what I told them: "Obey me, and I will be your God, and you will be my people. Do everything as I say, and all will be well!"

126. I Will Help You Get Back Up Again

You may be going through something that feels like it is more than you can handle. When your heart is weary, come to me and I will bring you rest. I know how hard you are trying to press through and fight this battle through prayer. It is working, because as you reach out to me I am giving you tools through my Spirit to make it through each day no matter what it holds.

I am here to refresh you and give you a renewed spirit. I am working deep within your heart to transform you into my image and likeness. Be perfect as your Father in heaven is perfect. Oh yes, I know this is a high calling, but you can make perfect choices as you follow my ways and calling upon your life.

Each time you meet with opposition, you have the opportunity to make the right choice. If you are unsure of what the right choice is, just come to me and I will guide your path. I want you to know this hour that I am proud of you and that I love you beyond compare.

I know that at times the road has been extremely difficult for you to travel upon. Remember that I am walking this road right alongside of you. If you trip and stumble, do not worry—do not condemn yourself as the enemy would want you to do. Just reach out your hand to me and I will help you get back up again. I will pour out my love and grace upon your life in new and amazing ways.

Your life is your testimony to others and when you overcome your battles and are still singing my praises—it is then that the power within you that comes from me will shine a light into the darkness of other people's lives. Your strength, perseverance, and fortitude come from me, my Child.

Each time you persevere through difficult times, you are one step closer to your victory through me. If you feel beat up on today from those who have hurt you or crushed your spirit with unkind words or acts, just come to me and I will speak words of life to you that will lift you up and give you new strength for your day.

Know this—I am with you. I am for you. I love you. That, my Child, will never change. Go forth now into your day with a new spring in your step and joy in your heart just by knowing and believing in your heart that I am with you. My peace I give to you now. Rest in me.

James 1:2-4
Dear brothers and sisters, when troubles of any kind
come your way, consider it an opportunity for great
joy. For you know that when your faith is tested, your
endurance has a chance to grow. So let it grow, for
when your endurance is fully developed, you will be
perfect and complete, needing nothing.

127. I Have Come to Set You Free

O h, how great is my love for you! When your world is falling apart all around you, turn your eyes toward your Maker. I will pick up the shattered pieces and put them back together in perfect order.

You have battle wounds from all the pain and heartache that you have experienced—I know this. But there is a hope you have in me to restore and rebuild your life to a state that is better than it was before you entered into your great trials.

I am sending my greatest warrior angels to fight on your behalf—to slay the enemy and put him under your feet. The enemy may at times get a foothold on you, but as you call upon my name I will loose you from his grip.

Every time you utter my Word from your lips, walls will start to fall down. I am giving you access to the mysteries of my kingdom that will guide you and enlighten your mind to the truth that will set you free from the bondage you have been in.

Be not weary, my Child; be courageous and boldly walk into new uncharted territories that I am giving you access to as you spend time in my presence. New hope I am sending your way to help build up your spirit and bring you new strength to face your daily battles.

It will not always be this difficult for you to overcome the enemy. I am teaching you the way, the truth, and the life every time you turn your eyes toward me. Rest assured I will go before you and make your path straight. Be encouraged this day and know that I have come to set the captives free. I have come to set you free.

You will be victorious for I have already won this battle you are facing. In time, your victory will manifest itself in your life and you will behold my greatness. You will come to understand more clearly how much I love you.

I am your Comforter. I am your Provider. I am your King and Savior. I am bringing you into a new day where you will feel my presence in new and mighty ways that will enable you to help others who are going through similar battles.

My peace I give you this day. Rest in my love. My love conquers all.

Romans 8:20-22
Against its will, all creation was subjected to God's curse. But with eager hope, the creation looks forward to the day when it will join God's children in glorious freedom from death and decay. For we know that all creation has been groaning as in the pains of childbirth right up to the present time.

128. I Have Called You to Be a Light to This World

You, my Child, are of great value to my kingdom. Others may not appreciate you for all the effort you put forth during each day but I appreciate you. I see the hidden things that others do not see. I see all that you do on behalf of others and know all the intents of your heart. I see you go about your day doing things to please those whom you love.

Even if it goes unnoticed by them, it does not go unnoticed by me. I notice every little act of kindness and generosity you give in thought and in deed—even the tiniest thoughts of love you express in your mind for others.

You are beautiful to me. You are my masterpiece. You radiate my light with every whisper of love that pours out of your heart to me and to those I have placed in your life.

You are here for a purpose—this day, this hour, this minute. I have called you to be a light to this world. I have chosen you. You are set apart and glorious in my eyes because you are my child.

I will help you today with anything that you need help with—just call on me. I will always give you what you need to accomplish my will for your life. Take notice of the little gifts I send you throughout the day.

Beloved, you make my heart smile every time you show me your love by loving others. Thank you for your faithfulness to me. I am always here for you.

Matthew 5:14
You are the light of the world—like a city on a hilltop that cannot be hidden.

129. Believe for a Greater Day!

*W*henever you hit a roadblock or obstacle that you can't seem to find your way around, look to me. I will go before you and make your path straight. Come to me for direction and I will lead the way.

Look not at the troubles you are in—look to me. I am bigger than your troubles and have the power to overcome them as you keep your eyes on me.

Believe for a greater day! It is coming. Hope for a brighter tomorrow! It is on its way. Pray for a miracle! I will answer.

Psalm 46:1
God is our refuge and strength, always ready to help
in times of trouble.

130. Let Not Your Heart Be Troubled

*L*et not your heart be troubled, my Child. I have come so that you may have rest. I am here for you today. Just call on me and I will answer. Let my peace rest upon your shoulders as you give all your worries and concerns to me.

It may feel as though there is no end to your trial, as if the weight of this world is going to crush you and you can barely breathe. This too shall pass, my Beloved. I am your strength as you persevere through this trial. I am building a new strength of character within you that will one day serve you well in the ministry I have called you to.

Yes, there is a plan I have for your life, a plan that will bring you the joy and peace you have been longing for. A plan where I will use you and these current circumstances for my glory to bring light to this broken world. The end of this trial you are in is drawing near. Keep hanging on.

I will bring you through this and you will be victorious in this battle for I am with you. I am on your side. The outcome may be different than what you expected, but in time you will begin to understand that this was all part of a greater plan.

Because of the darkness the enemy brings on this world you live in there are things that happen to my children that are not fair, that bring much pain and suffering. I know and understand your suffering for I too suffered. But ultimately through my suffering I paved a way for you to have victory over the enemy.

This life you live is but a blink of an eye in comparison to the eternal life I have for you because you have believed in me. You can make it. Be strong for the reward for your suffering is great—far greater than you could ever imagine.

I am storing up treasures in heaven for you with each tear that you cry. Continue to put all your faith and trust in me, in the promises I have given you in my Word. All will be well, my Beloved. All will be well. I have come so that you may have life and have it in abundance.

Romans 5:3-5
We can rejoice, too, when we run into problems and trials, for we know that they help us develop endurance. And endurance develops strength of character, and character strengthens our confident hope of salvation. And this hope will not lead to disappointment. For we know how dearly God loves us, because he has given us the Holy Spirit to fill our hearts with his love.

131. I Am Calling You to Come Away with Me

S weet Friend of my heart—I am drawing you closer to my heart in these last days. In the not too distant future, I will be returning to call all of my children home to their eternal resting place. In the meantime, stand strong and fight the good fight of faith.

I am pouring out my Spirit upon the lost and the broken children who are looking for guidance in their time of need. Rest assured that when I return, your life will transcend to a place you could have never even imagined or comprehended. You will be fully embraced in love with absolutely no evil to keep you from an eternal place of peace.

My hand is extended toward you and I am calling you to come away with me this day and spend some uninterrupted time with me. I have much to share with you.

I know that sometimes you feel like you are talking to a wall and that you do not hear a response from me or an answer to your prayers. That is far from the truth, for I am always listening and am always whispering words of wisdom to your spirit—though you are not always aware this is taking place.

The answers are happening all around you as you are led to take a step in the right direction by following after me. You do not have to know what is coming in the future—you just need to keep on trusting in me and my promises will manifest themselves in your life, oftentimes in ways you weren't even expecting.

You are doing well, my Child. It is an honor for me that you would take time out of your day to come and talk with me. Every time you call upon my name during the day, I come running to you with arms wide open.

Be at peace this hour and rest in the comfort of my love. I love you—I always have and I always will—that, my Beloved, will never change.

2 Timothy 4:7-8
I have fought the good fight, I have finished the race, and I have remained faithful. And now the prize awaits me—the crown of righteousness, which the Lord, the righteous Judge, will give me on the day of his return. And the prize is not just for me but for all who eagerly look forward to his appearing.

132. With All That I Am, I Love You

B e at peace this day and know that I love you. Let the greatness of my love for you sink into the fiber of your being. With all that I am, I love you. You know me because you have believed in me and because of this I have found a place in your heart to call my home.

Enter the gates of praise within you and sing out a new song of celebration! You were once lost but I found you, and you became a child of God to whom all my blessings flow. Now, it is my job as your one true Father to protect you, to lead you, to provide for you, and to love you into my eternal kingdom in which you will ultimately live in my house, your everlasting resting place.

Come away with me, my Beloved! Now that you have found me, I will never let you go.

Psalm 145:13
For your kingdom is an everlasting kingdom. You rule
throughout all generations. The Lord always keeps his
promises; he is gracious in all he does.

133. My Promises Are Coming at the Perfect Time

Be patient, my Child, I know that you are waiting for my promises to be fulfilled in your life. They are coming in my perfect time. You will one day look back on your life and be able to see that I never left your side. And when you share this with others, you will be giving glory to my Father who loves you beyond compare.

Thank you for persevering even when you have had little strength. I am your greatest advocate and I overflow with joy each time you call upon my name. I will always be faithful—this you can count on!

Romans 5:3-5
We can rejoice, too, when we run into problems and trials, for we know that they help us develop endurance. And endurance develops strength of character, and character strengthens our confident hope of salvation. And this hope will not lead to disappointment. For we know how dearly God loves us, because he has given us the Holy Spirit to fill our hearts with his love.

134. Forgive Others Who Have Done You Wrong

*B*eloved Sons and Daughters—behold, I bring you a new day! Rise up with a new fervor to praise my holy name and be a light unto the darkness. As you stand before me, I will pour over you new insight and revelation into the mysteries of my kingdom. As you take in all that I long to share with you, it will draw you closer to my heart.

There is not one place better to be than in my presence. It is in my presence that the heavens open up upon you and light your path. The angels are singing my praises in your midst every time you call upon my name. Be not weary of doing good, for great is your reward when you extend a helping hand and bring your love to others.

My love for you is like a consuming fire that keeps on burning brighter and brighter with greater intensity as each minute passes. I love you more and more every moment of your life that goes by. I am loving you into my eternal kingdom.

If only those people with hardened hearts would heed my call upon their life there would be so much more goodness in the land. What I ask of you this day is to turn away from evil and choose to do good.

Forgive others who have done you wrong, and great healing will take place in your heart and bring you freedom from your current internal struggles that battle within your heart and mind. If you cannot find it in your heart to forgive everyone, not just some—then come to me, ask me to help you and I will soften your heart.

Be light as I am light and it will be well with your soul. I will always show you my love—I give it to you pressed down, shaken together, and overflowing. Rest in my love this day and you will experience peace. My refreshing rain will heal any brokenness inside.

Matthew 6:14-15
If you forgive those who sin against you, your
heavenly Father will forgive you. But if you refuse to
forgive others, your Father will not forgive your sins.

135. In the Center of My Heart Is Where You Belong

*B*eloved, I am standing by your side this day. I am ready to work on your behalf as you call upon my name. When you get fatigued, I will rejuvenate your spirit as you ask me to. Allow me into your life in deeper ways.

I want you to really get to know who I am—who your Creator, Redeemer, and Savior is. If you really understood who your God is you would have no fears, doubts, or worries because I am always faithful.

I know and understand that this world is plagued by darkness because of people who turn their backs on me and deny my name. You also have the enemy working against you—spiritual warfare taking place. This can make your walk difficult.

Be patient and continue to trust in me and it will go well with you. You, my Child, do not deny me and therefore I will not deny you—in fact, I will lift you up. It is my job to show you the way to go.

Continue to talk to me throughout your day and I will move mountains for you. You will begin to recognize me and my presence in your life in new ways.

I am your greatest admirer and your greatest advocate. I am the best friend you will ever know and I am never going to leave your side as you continue to walk with me and walk in obedience and righteousness—this is what I ask of you.

When you go astray, I will come and find you and bring you back home where you belong—in the center of my heart. Trust in me today in everything you do and I will promote you and give you favor among men.

I am proud of you and I love you. Go forth and sing a new song in your heart today—I am listening and singing along with you!

Psalm 86:11-13
Teach me your ways, O Lord, that I may live according to your truth! Grant me purity of heart, so that I may honor you. With all my heart I will praise you, O Lord my God. I will give glory to your name forever, for your love for me is very great. You have rescued me from the depths of death.

136. I Know It Is Difficult to Slay Those Negative Thoughts

My Friend, listen to that still, small voice within your heart as my Spirit joins with yours in prayer. I have many things to share with you this day. You can always count on me to be there for you. I know what is coming in your life before it arrives, so it will serve you well to seek me for guidance to help you maneuver through your day successfully.

When you look to the past, only do so as a way to learn through me different ways you could have handled a situation so that when similar circumstances arise you will have a better path to take. Do not berate yourself for things that have gone wrong or things you have done wrong. Just simply seek my forgiveness and I will forgive you. From that point on the slate has been wiped clean and you can begin again fresh on your next journey.

The enemy will continue to try to point the finger at your mistakes and make you feel embarrassed and humiliated. Do not let him do this for it will only bring you down and rob you of the many gifts I want to bless you with. I know it is difficult to slay those negative thoughts for they can be very strong.

Something I would suggest to you in these moments is to lift up your voice in song to praise the Father—just a sweet simple tune that you make up or one that you already know. The song does not matter, it's the act of praising my Father that will change the atmosphere around you and get you centered back in on the truth of my love.

Be at peace this day and know that I love you beyond compare. There is so much goodness coming your way!

Psalm 59:17
O my Strength, to you I sing praises, for you, O God,
are my refuge, the God who shows me unfailing love.

137. No Matter What You Are Facing, We Can Tackle It Together

S weet Friend, Beloved of my heart—do not worry about what is going to happen today. Put all your faith and trust in me. That is the very best thing you can do—the only solution that will truly make a difference in the outcome of your day.

What you have before you today is all you can work on at this moment in time. You cannot skip a day or days ahead. You need to be present in the moment yet filled with hope for the future—hope that you *can* achieve your dreams, that you *will* receive the desires of your heart, and that you *will* be free from the bondage or trial you are in.

We can only take it one day at a time together. If I were to give you five days to take on at once you would be overwhelmed and overburdened. I give you this one day to work on.

No matter what you are facing, we can tackle it together. You will be successful as you lean on me with all your heart. Remember, my yoke is easy and my burden is light. I will not give you more than you can handle. I will always be your strength as you call upon my name.

Psalm 55:22
Give your burdens to the Lord, and he will take care
of you. He will not permit the godly to slip and fall.

138. When All of a Sudden Something Knocks You off Course

*D*earest Beloved Child of mine, Friend of my heart—seek me in all your daily activities and you will find me. Remember to smile—a simple smile can bring a little extra joy to your spirit and will light a spark in others who see it. I have called you to be a light. Where there is my light, there cannot be darkness for my light overpowers the darkness.

Press forward and stand strong when the enemy tries to get in your way. Some days you will be going about just fine when all of a sudden something knocks you off course and robs your peace. If you realize that it is simply the enemy trying to steal something from you, you have the power to take back what he robbed from you that moment by calling on my name.

In the midst of the fire, I will come along beside you and shield you from the flames. My Word is a very powerful tool when you are battling the enemy who is trying to drag you down. My Word is a mighty sword that will slay those thoughts of negativity that the enemy tries to bog your mind down with.

When you recognize the power of my Word, you will realize how much strength it will give you. That is my tool for you to use on a daily basis in addition to prayer and communion with me. Do not fear when the enemy throws a rock in your direction because I have come to remove that obstacle or change the course of your path.

Today, lift up your heart in praise and I will send my greatest angels to fight on your behalf. You will be victorious in me and through me.

John 10:10
The thief's purpose is to steal and kill and destroy. My
purpose is to give them a rich and satisfying life.

139. You Are Closer to Freedom than You Can Imagine

I have come so that you may have new life, a life free from bondages. When you feel backed into a corner and you don't know how to escape, call upon my name and I will come running to you. You have felt the wounds that have come from the attacks of the enemy. Talk to me about them. Reach within and express your deepest thoughts and concerns. I sit right by your side and am listening to you.

My healing rains, in their mysterious ways, will wash away the hurts and pain. I will help you to sort out your thoughts and bring them into alignment with my will for your life. I will help you to forgive others who have hurt you deeply. You will recover and you will become stronger than ever before.

Be patient with yourself and listen to the promptings of my Spirit which will lead the way. You are closer to freedom than you can imagine. I have new blessings awaiting you this day.

2 Corinthians 3:17
For the Lord is the Spirit, and wherever the Spirit of
the Lord is, there is freedom.

140. I Will Strengthen You

Today, seek after me. Call upon my name and I will answer. I will put a new song in your heart and give you a greater fervor to accomplish the tasks that are before you.

Whenever you come up against a situation that is causing you to question your own ability to perform—be confident that I will carry you through. I want for you to trust in me. I am your guide. I am your helper.

My Spirit within you will enlighten you and give you a greater understanding of the power of my Word and how it can help you to overcome any negative thoughts that may come your way. The enemy likes to get into your thought life and make you feel as though you are inadequate—to make you feel like you do not have what it takes to do the task at hand.

When you go about your work, whenever you are burdened down by negative thoughts—remember that you are my Child. You are my Beloved. You do have what it takes to do the job because I am always with you. I will strengthen you and give you a fresh new confidence in yourself.

Sing the new song I have placed in your heart today and you will experience peace and calm during stressful situations. I am going to do a new thing in your heart this day. Be ready to receive new wisdom from me—new ways of looking at things.

Rest in my love today. I am standing right by your side.

Psalm 31:24
So be strong and courageous, all you who put your
hope in the Lord!

141. I Am Fighting on Your Behalf for Your Freedom

*T*oday as you go about your day, be mindful to call upon my name whenever you come up against something you don't know how to handle. I will point you in the right direction. Also, come to me when you feel discouraged and I will encourage you by bringing people to you who will speak life into your situation.

This life of yours is not always going to be easy; on the contrary, you will hit many roadblocks along the way. But have no fear, for I will always give you a way out—another road to travel on to get you to your destination right on time.

I know you can get frustrated with me about the timing of events in your life. I understand this and want you to know that I always work things out for your very best interest. There are some roads you travel upon that you may think are the way you should be traveling, but if you were to be able to see farther down the road you would find that that particular road may lead to more pain and heartache.

Sometimes you end up down that road of pain and heartache because you lost your way. In those times, call on me and I will show you the way to the highway that leads to life—a life full of abundance, a life full of love. I am fighting on your behalf for your freedom—freedom from a life of bondage, unhealthy habits, negative thinking, and all the things that keep you from reaching your full potential through me.

As you are set free and the chains that bind you are broken, you will begin to see your current situation with fresh new eyes. I will transform your mind and heart and help you to align your life with my most perfect, good, and pleasing will.

The battle you are facing now will not break you but only make you stronger. You will get through this. No matter how long it takes to fight the battle—put all your trust in me. Know that the battle has already been won—you just may not see it this present day.

I leave you with one parting thought this hour. When you are feeling weary, lift up your voice in song to praise your heavenly Father who has given you life. I sit by my Father's side and go to Him daily on your behalf. As you sing praises to my Father, His heart is turned with compassion toward you and you will find increasing favor flow upon your life.

Be of good cheer this day for I am near. I am with you. I love you. Let's travel down this journey of life together hand in hand all the way.

> *Deuteronomy 20:4*
> *For the Lord your God is going with you! He will fight*
> *for you against your enemies, and he will give you*
> *victory!*

142. You Do Matter

I see the sorrow in your heart. Be not dismayed, for I am with you always. In this time of loneliness and despair I want you to remember that you can count on me to be faithful to my promises that I speak of in my Word. The truth is that I will never leave you nor forsake you. As you go about your day be mindful to open up your heart to receive my love.

Sometimes life makes you feel as though you are gasping for air, as if the walls are closing in on you, as if your hope is growing dim. Rest assured that I am here to light your path. I am here to bring you new hope. I am here to comfort you.

When you begin your day, as your day is in motion, and when your day is coming to a close, seek me and you will find me—even in places you were not expecting. You are a priceless treasure to me—a masterpiece—one of a kind.

Perhaps you are feeling this hour that your life does not matter, that it has no meaning, and that you don't have anything to offer others because you are in so much pain yourself. Let me take the burden of those thoughts off of your shoulders.

Because you are my Child you do matter. Because you are my Child your life does have meaning. Although you feel you don't have the energy to give, you have a giving heart and I honor that with my love for you.

When you love me and pour out your heart to me in prayer, I will give you what you need to make it through your day. You may feel as though you can't make it through today. You will make it through because I will help you. As you come to me for answers I am here to respond in loving kindness. Sweet child, you are beloved in my eyes.

Go forth now into this day and remember that I gave my very life for you so that you may rise up to a new life in me. It will not always be easy; in fact, you will at times run into obstacles, roadblocks which you don't know how you can get around. I will remove those obstacles for you when that is needed. Consider this—the roadblock may be there for your own good though you may not understand why at this present time. You will in days to come.

Lift your heart to me in prayer this hour and I will come running to your aid. I love you. I adore you. I give you my heart and all that I have to offer. I will renew your spirit and strengthen your mind to fight the good fight. You will be victorious for you always have God on your side.

Isaiah 54:12
I will make your towers of sparkling rubies,
your gates of shining gems, and your walls of
precious stones.

143. I Bring You a New Day

*B*eloved Child, behold, I bring you a new day! Today I will open your eyes to see new ways I am working in your life from the sounds of the birds chirping when you arise to the warm glow of the setting sun as the day is put to rest. It pleases my heart to see you look at your surroundings—at the beauty of my creation—to see your thankfulness for all that I bless you with each day.

Some days you become so busy that you don't take time to be aware of your surroundings. Be mindful to take moments of pause throughout your day and go out and breathe in a breath of fresh air. Look up at the sky whether there be clouds or sunshine or a beautiful mix of both.

My creation—this planet upon which you live—is my gift for you to treasure. I have blessed you with much and have so many more blessings I am waiting to pour out upon your life. As you go about your day today, make an effort to reach out to people with kindness in your heart, even if you are brushed off by someone with a cold attitude.

When you are kind to people, you are planting seeds of kindness in their hearts. When you are loving to people, you are planting seeds of love in their heart. I am planting fruitful seeds of love in your heart which will help you to love yourself more and to love those people I have placed in your life.

Sing a new song in your heart today as you praise your Father in heaven. I am listening and am embracing you with my love. Go forth into this new day and live according to my purpose with a fragrant love in your heart that flows out of you to all my dear children that you pass by. Always remember, I love you so.

Psalm 65:8
Those who live at the ends of the earth stand in awe
of your wonders. From where the sun rises to where it
sets, you inspire shouts of joy.

144. Pass the Torch

When the road is rocky and you have lost your footing, reach out your hand to me and I will smooth out the path before you. Rest assured this day that no matter what comes your way, you will be victorious as you continue to put all your faith and trust in me. As you put your trust in me, I will fill your spirit with new hope that lifts you up and helps you accomplish the task at hand more effectively and bring peace to your heart.

Today, as I draw my children to you—speak life over them and build up their spirit with encouraging, life-giving words. You have what it takes to make a great difference in the lives of others. So many people are lost and lonely. It only takes one positive word to build a person's esteem for the day. Remember that people want to be noticed and to be loved and appreciated.

Take an extra moment to thank someone for the efforts you see they are putting forth at the task at hand. You are a light to my children as I am in you and I am light.

Pass the torch! Build up the body of Christ this day as you look for the good in others. Edify them by giving them words of encouragement. As you encourage others, you will bring a spring to their step and joy to their heart. As you lift up your friends by walking with a positive attitude, more will get accomplished for my kingdom today.

Take a moment this hour to reflect on my goodness. I am with you and I am for you. Always trust in me. I will never let you down.

Matthew 5:16
***In the same way, let your good deeds shine out for
all to see, so that everyone will praise your heavenly
Father.***

145. You Are My Champion

*D*earest Beloved Child of mine—look into my eyes and let me tell you how much I love you. You are so dear to my heart. As you go about your day, take moments of pause to think about your God who loves you beyond compare.

When you hit a bump in the road, call upon my name and I will smooth out the road you are traveling on so that you can get to your destination successfully and right on time. You are making your way through life like a champion. You are my champion. It may not seem that way to you at this present time, but just the fact that you are here with me now is building that champion spirit within you.

I am preparing the way for you to reach your destiny. I have a call upon your life and a plan for you that will bring you great joy in the days to come. Trust in me and I will reveal it to you.

Send up a prayer to your Father in heaven. He eagerly anticipates the moments when you call on Him. Your Father in heaven is so proud of you. I am proud of you. Walk in obedience before your God and you will be greatly blessed. I am sending many blessings your way. Keep your eyes open to see all that I am doing in your life.

Lean on me when you are feeling weak and I will strengthen you. My peace I give to you this hour. Let me wrap you in a blanket of my love and you will feel the comfort you have been longing for.

Be of good cheer, for I am sending you down a new path of greatness. I will always be your guide.

Psalm 73:24
You guide me with your counsel, leading me to a
glorious destiny.

146. I Will Comfort You

*T*oday as you call upon my name, I will answer. I long to have you sit in my presence. Rejoice, for a new day is dawning! Tomorrow will be full of new experiences and you will receive insight into how I am working in your life. When you are seeking me for answers, you will find me. When you ask me, I will respond accordingly to my perfect will for your life.

You are a prized pearl in my kingdom. I treasure you. I cherish you because you are my Beloved Child with whom I am well pleased.

Don't let a day pass by without looking up to me. I am always looking down upon you, watching you, comforting you, and reassuring you that all will be well.

I know there are times when you are looking for answers, but no matter how hard you try to find them, they seem nowhere to be found.

You may even find that the answer you were looking for is not the answer you were hoping for.

I do not ask more of you than to love me, to love others, and to walk in obedience. Just know that I have a perfect reason for answering the way that I do. Trust in me, for my plan for you is perfect. Sometimes you slip and fall but I am always by your side ready to pick you up and send you down a brighter, more rewarding path.

As you begin your day, call upon my name. I will be with you every moment no matter what comes your way!

Psalm 10:17
*Lord, you know the hopes of the helpless. Surely you
will hear their cries and comfort them.*

147. Keep Pressing Forward

*E*nter into prayer this night with an open heart. Allow all the concerns and worries of the day to fade away and press in to hear my voice. I have so much to share with you. Be patient with yourself as I am patient with you.

Some days you will run into situations that will cause you to stumble. Do not look back, keep pressing forward. And if you do look back, ask me to help you, look upon that situation through my eyes and I will show you different ways to handle similar circumstances.

I have a day full of blessings to bring to you when you arise in the morning. Every time you call upon my name, I come running to you with arms wide open. I eagerly anticipate the times you come and talk with me.

I want to be your very best friend. I am the most faithful friend you will ever know and I always stick to my promises. I always have and I always will. I promise to love you always—that will never change.

Lift up your hands in praise to the Father and I will shower down upon you healing rains that will renew your spirit and refresh your mind. Be confident and trust in me always. I am with you now.

Philippians 3:14
I press on to reach the end of the race and receive the
heavenly prize for which God, through Christ Jesus, is
calling us.

148. I Will Lead You to the Mountaintop

Beloved Child, when you are weary, come to me and I will give you rest. The burden of this day may be weighing you down but I want you to know that as you let me lift your worries and concerns off of your shoulders you will begin to feel renewed and refreshed. It pleases my heart to know that you love me and that you desire to follow after me.

The road will not always be easy; on the contrary, for those who follow me the road is narrow but the reward is great and it will be worth it all in the end. I have been with you in your sufferings. I have wiped the tears of your sorrow.

I know that there are some things in life that seem to be too big to handle, but you do not have to walk this journey alone. As long as you are seeking after me, even in those times where you can't seem to figure out what to do, just trust in me and I will make a way for you in the wilderness. I will always be the light in the darkness.

I will shine my light upon your path so that each step you take will be more secure and you will become stronger and stronger the farther up the mountain you go. As you look to the mountaintop you may find that a cloud is blocking the view of the mountain peak. You believe in your heart that it is still there but you just can't see it today so you keep pressing forward. That is faith. That is your hope that keeps you moving forward to a brighter day.

Keep stepping out in faith and I will lead you to the mountaintop where you will once again bask in the glory of my light. Come to me, my Beloved—I have so much to share with you.

Matthew 7:14
But the gateway to life is very narrow and the road is difficult, and only a few ever find it.

149. This Suffering Is Only Temporary

*M*y Beloved Child, here I am in your midst. I stand right by your side. Take me by the hand and let me show you new things, things you've not yet considered. There are many paths to take in life but there is one perfect path that I have chosen for you. The path you are on may be difficult, but trust me that I will lead you in the right direction as you continue to look to me for guidance.

The path you are on may be filled with thorn bushes and weeds, which are making it challenging to walk forward. Do not lose hope, for on the other side of the thorn bush is a beautiful rose. I will show you how to find the rose.

Do not cast your thoughts forward worrying about the future. Rest in the present where I am speaking to your heart. Tomorrow will be here before you know it, but today is where I want to teach you new things.

I want to talk to you about the trial you are going through and help you to understand how keeping your faith in me while going through challenges is drawing you closer to my heart. It is in these times that I am molding you into my image and likeness and perfecting your heart.

Have hope, my Child. This suffering is only temporary; remember the rose. The pain will pass and a new day is on the horizon. Rejoice in your hope. There you will find joy amidst the sorrow.

Rest in my heart now and I will bring you the comfort your heart is longing for. My peace I am singing over you now. Embrace it with arms wide open.

Psalm 25:4-5
Show me the right path, O Lord; point out the road for
me to follow. Lead me by your truth and teach me,
for you are the God who saves me. All day long I put
my hope in you.

150. I Will Work with You as Your Teammate and Coach

*D*earest Beloved, I know you have a lot on your plate right now. Come to me and I will work with you as your teammate and coach. I will help you accomplish your tasks this day. Do not worry. We will get through this together.

When anxious thoughts race through your head, turn to me. I will remind you that you can do all things through me. As you go about your day, remember to talk to me. Share what's on your heart—your worries, your concerns, and your doubts. I will refresh your spirit and build your confidence. I will guide you to my Word that will help strengthen you.

Be of good cheer this day! There may be a lot going on, but you are not in this alone. We're a team and together we will accomplish my perfect will for your day.

Isaiah 26:3
You will keep in perfect peace all who trust in you, all whose thoughts are fixed on you!

151. Never Have I Been so Proud to Call You My Beloved

My heart leaps with you every time you come running to me! I have so much love and goodness to pour into you. Receive my love with arms wide open. I am wrapping a blanket of love and perfect peace around your heart this day. Do not fear what lies ahead. I already have a plan.

I want you to rest here and now in the presence of my love. Let me sing words of grace and mercy over your heart. Let me fill your mind with good thoughts. Let me shine a light in the darkness and fill you so full of my love that you are ready to explode with your heart on fire to love others.

In your darkest hours, I have held your hand and wiped your tears. When you have been afraid, I have held you in my arms and protected you. When you are worried, I speak to your spirit words of peace that quiet your soul.

Never have I been so proud to call you my Beloved. Arise, my Beloved, and come away with me! I want you to see the world through my eyes. I will be with you today. Take my hand and walk with me and talk with me. I've got everything under control. I am perfect love and I love you beyond compare.

Psalm 66:5
Come and see what our God has done, what awesome
miracles he performs for people!

Romans 15:13
I pray that God, the source of hope, will fill you
completely with joy and peace because you trust in
him. Then you will overflow with confident hope
through the power of the Holy Spirit.

About the Author

*D*ana Howard is simply one woman who loves the Lord Jesus Christ with all her heart and has a great passion to share God's love with the world. She has experienced huge trials in her life, and her relationship with God carried her through to a place of freedom, peace, and joy. She wants people to know this is possible for everyone who comes to know Jesus as their personal Savior and Friend. Dana lives in Washington State with her husband and is the mother of three boys. She works full time as a staff analyst and works on writing and her Facebook ministry, The Peace of Heaven, in her spare time. Her mission is to inspire people to draw closer to the heart of God through writing words of encouragement and prayers that the Lord impresses upon her heart. Contact Dana at www.dreamingofjesus.com.

CPSIA information can be obtained
at www.ICGtesting.com
Printed in the USA
LVOW04s0347050117
519815LV00034B/514/P

9 780692 455562